EXTREME HOCKEY TRIVIA

GREYSTONE BOOKS

Douglas & McIntyre Publishing Group

Vancouver/Toronto/New York

For Karen and Rob: our linemates (and lawn mates) on Hingston Street.

— Don Weekes

Greystone Books
A division of Douglas & McIntyre Ltd.
2323 Quebec Street, Suite 201
Vancouver, British Columbia   V5T 4S7

Canadian Cataloguing in Publication Data
Weekes, Don.
  Extreme hockey trivia
  ISBN 1-55054-711-9
  1. Hockey—Miscellanea.   2. National Hockey League—Miscellanea.
I. Title.
GV847.W362 1999   796.962'64   C99-910624-4

Editing by Anne Rose and Kerry Banks
Design by Peter Cocking
Typesetting by Brenda and Neil West, BN Typographics West
Cover photo by Bruce Bennett/Bruce Bennett Studios
Printed and bound in Canada by Transcontinental Printing/Imprimerie Gagne
Printed on acid-free paper ∞

The publisher gratefully acknowledges the assistance of the Canada Council for the Arts and of the British Columbia Ministry of Tourism, Small Business and Culture. The publisher also acknowledges the financial support of the Government of Canada through the Book Publishing Industry Development Program for its publishing activities.

Canada

Don Weekes is a television producer and writer with CFCF 12 in Montreal. This is his thirteenth hockey trivia quiz book.

CONTENTS

PREFACE

They called him the Rocket. He was the great Maurice Richard, a giant in a game that has grown up around his scoring exploits and feats of brawn. Almost 40 years after he retired in 1960, the NHL officially recognized Richard's contributions to hockey by awarding the annual Maurice Richard Trophy to the year's leading goal scorer.

In a strange twist, the award's first winner, Teemu Selanne (in 1998-99), did not score 50 goals—Richard's most durable legacy. But Selanne's league-leading 47 goals in an 82-game schedule does put the Rocket's 1944-45 achievement of 50-in-50 in perspective for today's fans.

So who was hockey's original "Rocket"?

Perhaps it was old-timer Tom Johnson's story about playing in exhibition games with the great Richard that best describes the Rocket's enduring impact on hockey crowds. Johnson, an ex-Montreal teammate of Richard's during the 1950s, played with the Canadiens on barnstorming tours around Quebec. Players were always introduced by their numbers. Richard, of course, wore his famous No. 9 jersey, and Johnson, No. 10. As Johnson put it, no one ever knew who he was, because by the time the cheering died down for the Rocket the house announcer was already down to No. 14.

Johnson recalled this anecdote to broadcaster Dick Irvin during the closing ceremonies for the Montreal Forum in 1996. Richard had just been introduced and the crowd, most of whom had never seen him play, were standing and cheering in a six-minute ovation that "went on forever."

The Rocket hadn't scored a goal in 36 years, Dick Irvin observed. Yet, there he was, a legend in his 70s, still creating a little bit of Canadian lore.

There has never been a player whose image has lasted as long as Richard's. He played to the extreme. A five-time goal-scoring champion who, in the days before team enforcers, fought his own battles even though he was the NHL's biggest attraction. The Rocket paid for that privilege every night, with a disproportionate series of game misconducts, suspensions and fines for altercations with opponents and officials alike.

In this thirteenth book in our series on hockey trivia, we salute the playing of hockey to the extreme—the spirit that the Rocket embodied in his game. From the blueline in, no one deked and dazzled like Richard; his coal-black eyes glaring as he bore down on the net, sometimes carrying a 200-pound defenseman on his back. It was Richard's heart and desire that hockey fans so wildly saluted in 1996. His trophy is a monument to his singular passion: scoring goals. Long live the Rocket.

DON WEEKES
MAY 1999

Visit my Web site at: **www3.sympatico.ca/don.weekes/**

1

OPEN ICE

After years spent perfecting suffocating defense systems, coaches in the late 1990s began tinkering with strategies that would make their teams more creative offensively. The approach was successful, particularly in Toronto and Buffalo, where strong goaltending helped to counter the risk of allowing goals on breakaways or two-on-ones. Even Dallas and New Jersey, two trap-oriented teams, began pressing the attack more to create prime scoring chances. In this first chapter we open up the ice with some general hockey questions, to generate more offense and put a few points in the win column. Don't forget, it's not necessarily how much you know; luck and logic play a big part in any game plan.

(Answers are on page 6)

1.1   **What was the speed of the fastest shot on record during the 1990s?**
A. 98 miles per hour
B. 100 miles per hour
C. 102 miles per hour
D. 106 miles per hour

1.2   **Which team iced the "Bruise Brothers"?**
A. The Detroit Red Wings
B. The Philadelphia Flyers
C. The Boston Bruins
D. The Calgary Flames

1.3   **What helped cure Paul Kariya of his post-concussion symptoms in 1998?**
A. Psychoanalysis
B. Acupuncture
C. Hypnosis
D. A hyperbaric chamber

1.4 As of 1998-99, when was the last time a defenseman won the Hart Trophy as league MVP?
A. Bobby Orr in 1972
B. Denis Potvin in 1976
C. Rod Langway in 1984
D. Ray Bourque in 1990

1.5 How much money did Sandis Ozolinsh lose during his contract dispute with the Colorado Avalanche in 1998-99?
A. Between $100,000 and $500,000
B. Between $500,000 and $1 million
C. Between $1 million and $1½ million
D. More than $1½ million

1.6 If Wayne Gretzky scored his 500th goal in 575 games and Mike Bossy scored his 500th in 647 matches, in what career game did sniper Brett Hull record his 500th?
A. Brett's 593rd game
B. Brett's 643rd game
C. Brett's 693rd game
D. Brett's 743rd game

1.7 According to the NHL Players' Association, which arena has the best ice conditions?
A. The Canadian Airlines Saddledome in Calgary
B. The First Union Center in Philadelphia
C. The Molson Centre in Montreal
D. Edmonton's Skyreach Centre

1.8 What is the most common nickname in hockey?
A. Red
B. Mr. _____ (as in Mr. Goalie)
C. Flash
D. Moose

1.9 Who was Detroit coach Scotty Bowman targeting when he said, "The only thing he didn't do was win an Olympic medal. And I was kind of glad he didn't because we wouldn't have heard the end of it."
A. Chicago's Chris Chelios
B. Philadelphia's Eric Lindros
C. Colorado's Patrick Roy
D. Dallas' Brett Hull

1.10 Which forward line was considered the first power trio in the NHL?
A. The Montreal Maroons' S Line
B. Toronto's Kid Line
C. New York's A Line
D. Detroit's Production Line

1.11 Who is known as "Dr. Calipers" around the NHL?
A. A referee
B. A goalie equipment inspector
C. A video goal judge
D. A team doctor

1.12 How much money did Sergei Fedorov lose after being suspended five games for slashing Zdeno Chara during the 1998-99 season?
A. Between $1 and $100,000
B. Between $100,000 and $200,000
C. Between $200,000 and $300,000
D. More than $300,000

1.13 Which famous hockey incident did Canadian rockers the Tragically Hip write about in their song, "Fifty-Mission Cap"?
A. The 1923 disappearance of the Stanley Cup
B. The 1951 death of Toronto's Bill Barilko
C. The 1955 "Richard Riot" in Montreal
D. The 1972 Summit Series between Canada and Russia

1.14 Which tough guy owns the NHL record for most fights in a season?
A. Dave Williams
B. Mike Peluso
C. Tie Domi
D. Paul Laus

1.15 How many NHL regulars wore sweater No. 13 in 1998-99?
A. One player
B. Four players
C. Eight players
D. 16 players

1.16 Who is the Albanian Assassin?
A. Stu Grimson
B. Donald Brashear
C. Tie Domi
D. Rob Ray

1.17 Who was the first European-trained NHLer elected to the Hockey Hall of Fame?
A. Sweden's Borje Salming
B. The USSR's Vladislav Tretiak
C. Czechoslovakia's Peter Stastny
D. The USSR's Anatoli Tarasov

1.18 What is the NHL's all-time goals-per-game scoring average?
A. 4.12 goals per game
B. 6.12 goals per game
C. 8.12 goals per game
D. 10.2 goals per game

1.19 What kind of disciplinary action did Chicago's Reid Simpson receive after he threw a water bottle at a fan in November 1998?
A. A warning from the referee
B. A two-minute penalty
C. A game misconduct
D. A two-game suspension

1.20 Who was the first player in NHL history to score 100 points and record 100 penalty minutes in the same season?

A. Bobby Orr

B. Phil Esposito

C. Gordie Howe

D. Bobby Clarke

1.21 Who was the second European defenseman after Borje Salming to score 500 points in the NHL?

A. Sweden's Fredrik Olausson

B. The Czech Republic's Petr Svoboda

C. Russia's Sergei Zubov

D. Latvia's Sandis Ozolinsh

1.22 What national anthem was played when the Unified Team (so-called after the breakup of the USSR) won the gold medal in hockey at the 1992 Winter Olympics in Albertville, France?

A. The anthem of the USSR

B. The Olympic anthem

C. The new anthem of Russia

D. No anthem was played

1.23 How many millionaires were playing in the NHL in 1998-99?

A. Less than 100 millionaires

B. Between 100 and 150 millionaires

C. Between 150 and 200 millionaires

D. More than 200 millionaires

1.24 Considering that NHL ironman Doug Jarvis played a record 964 straight games and the league once played 44- and 48-game schedules during the 1920s and 1930s, how many consecutive games did the NHL's first ironman forward play during hockey's early days?

A. 308 consecutive games

B. 408 consecutive games

C. 508 consecutive games

D. 608 consecutive games

1.25 Which Chicago Blackhawk scored the last goal in Maple Leaf
Gardens history?
A. Doug Gilmour
B. Bob Probert
C. Reid Simpson
D. Tony Amonte

1.26 Which is the only family to have three brothers inducted into
the Hockey Hall of Fame?
A. The Patrick family
B. The Conacher family
C. The Richard family
D. The Cook family

1.27 What is slew-footing?
A. A term used in contract negotiations
B. An on-ice act of violence
C. A method of molding plastic skate boots
D. A practical joke played on rookies

OPEN ICE
Answers

1.1 **D. 106 miles per hour**
The NHL's elite can fire the puck in the 90- to 100-miles-per-
hour range (Al MacInnis clocked the hardest shot, 100.4 miles
per hour, at the 1999 NHL All-Star game). But Shawn Heins, a
little-known defenseman from Canada's national team, made
sports headlines in 1999 after launching a 106-miles-per-hour
missile in the skills competition at the U.S. Hockey League
All-Star game. Heins, six foot four and 220 pounds, used a
Bauer 3030, the same stick model as Eric Lindros's. "I have my
own pattern but it's basically the same stick as Lindros uses,
said Heins. "There is only a small curve on it, near the heel. But
it's a very heavy stick—that may generate some of the power.
More than anything, I think it's because it comes naturally,
something God-given, and I've worked hard on it." A classic

late bloomer, Heins, at age 25, saw his first NHL action with San Jose in February 1999.

1.2   A. The Detroit Red Wings
In Jake and Elwood Blues's hometown (Motown), Red Wing fans readily embraced the team's two toughest hit men—Bob Probert and Joe Kocur—and nicknamed them the Bruise Brothers. Together, Probert and Kocur forged a reputation as the NHL's best one-two punch on the same team. Probert, despite his struggle with substance abuse, became the league's undisputed heavyweight champion. Kocur was the strongest and meanest fighter on the ice, a goon with fists that packed the force of a runaway freight train. The Bruise Brothers' reign of terror in Detroit ended when Kocur was traded in 1991 and Probert in 1994.

1.3   B. Acupuncture
After being sidelined with a concussion for the last three months of the 1997-98 season and having to miss the Nagano Olympics, Kariya took Eric Lindros's advice and turned to acupuncture to help clear the fog. "I had needles all over me. I don't enjoy needles but these are very fine. And at that point I was for whatever helped." For the mightiest Duck, normal activities such as walking, or talking on the phone for any length of time, were impossible. After a month of treatments two or three times a week, the fuzziness and other symptoms disappeared. On the ice, Kariya followed Pat LaFontaine's recovery plan for post-concussion syndrome, and began wearing a customized helmet, chin strap and mouth guard to absorb the shock of blows to the head.

1.4   A. Bobby Orr in 1972
The Hart Trophy typically goes to the Gretzkys, Lemieuxs and Hulls, transcendent offensive players who almost single-handedly strengthen the production of the entire team during a season. Rarely have MVP honours been bestowed on members of the defensive corps. Ray Bourque? Denis Potvin? Neither have won it. In fact, only seven rearguards have ever had their names etched on the Hart—and only one of those won it in the last 50

years. The last D-man so recognized was Bobby Orr, a hockey icon who literally changed the game with his play, while capturing three consecutive Harts in 1970, 1971 and 1972. Prior to Orr, the Hart hadn't been claimed by a blueliner since 1943-44, when Babe Pratt set an NHL scoring record for rearguards with 57 points on 17 goals and 40 assists. In that early era, defensemen were regular MVP winners. Tom Anderson, a converted winger, was named league MVP on the last-place Brooklyn Americans and led all blueliners with 41 points in 1941-42; Ebbie Goodfellow, a one-time centre, captained the Red Wings and won the Hart in 1940; Eddie Shore, the best defenseman in his time, won four Harts with his rough-and-tumble game; Babe Siebert, a former left wing, anchored a weak Montreal team and led the Habs to a first-place finish; Herb Gardiner helped the Canadiens to the best defensive record in the NHL in 1926-27.

The NHL's MVP-Winning Defensemen*						
Player	Team	Year	GP	G	A	Pts
Bobby Orr	Boston	1972	76	37	80	117
Bobby Orr	Boston	1971	78	37	102	139
Bobby Orr	Boston	1970	76	33	87	120
Babe Pratt	Toronto	1944	50	17	40	57
Tom Anderson	Brooklyn	1942	48	12	29	41
Ebbie Goodfellow	Detroit	1940	43	11	17	28
Eddie Shore	Boston	1938	48	3	14	17
Babe Siebert	Montreal	1937	44	8	20	28
Eddie Shore	Boston	1936	45	3	16	19
Eddie Shore	Boston	1935	48	7	26	33
Eddie Shore	Boston	1933	48	8	27	35
Herb Gardiner	Montreal	1927	44	6	6	12
* Current to 1998-99						

1.5   C. **Between $1 million and $1½ million**
Ozolinsh, one of the NHL's top offensive defensemen, lost more than $1 million in salary after negotiations with Colorado general manager Pierre Lacroix bogged down in early 1998-99. Lacroix played hardball throughout the negotiations, but finally signed Ozolinsh to a $6.7-million, two-year contract. On a

prorated basis for the 38 games he missed, Ozolinsh was paid $2.9 million in his first year. That cost him about $1.3 million in lost revenues. Ozolinsh received $3.8 million in the second year, just below the $4 million he was holding out for. The Latvian D-man said he had no problem with the forfeited income. "It was basically principle," said Ozolinsh. For the Avalanche, the new contract was worth it. Sparked by his return, Colorado went on a club-record 12-game winning streak. Ozolinsh then suffered a bruised sternum and missed three games. The Avs went 0-2-1 without him.

1.6 C. Brett's 693rd game

Hull notched his 500th against Los Angeles' Stephane Fiset on December 22, 1996, in a 7-4 St. Louis win over the Kings. He recorded the fourth-fastest 500th goal in league annals, behind Wayne Gretzky, Mario Lemieux and Mike Bossy.

The NHL's Fastest 500-Goal Scorers*			
Player	**Team**	**Date**	**Game No.**
Wayne Gretzky	Edm	11/22/86	575
Mario Lemieux	Pit	10/26/95	605
Mike Bossy	NYI	01/02/86	647
Brett Hull	St.L	12/22/96	693
Phil Esposito	Bos	12/22/74	803
Jari Kurri	LA	10/17/92	833
Bobby Hull	Chi	02/21/70	861
Marcel Dionne	LA	12/14/82	887
*Current to 1998-99			

1.7 D. Edmonton's Skyreach Centre

Long considered a league-wide problem, excellent ice conditions exist at only a few arenas. The best, according to most NHL players, is at Skyreach Centre, where the ice is made as hard and as thin as possible without being brittle. (Thin ice is harder because the cooling agents in the floor are closer to the ice surface.) Hard ice means less friction, which produces greater speed, crisp passing and more responsive skating. Another reason the ice is superior in Edmonton is the Zamboni blades that are used. They are sharpened twice a week (compared to once a month in other buildings) to give a fine and fast ice finish. While league representatives inspect arenas and work with staff to try and improve their ice, some facilities, such as New York's Madison Square Garden and the Continental Airlines Arena in New Jersey, still have terrible playing surfaces.

1.8 A. Red

Some 17 hockey men have been called Red, by far the most common nickname in the game. Best known are Red Kelly, Red Berenson, Red Storey and Red Sullivan.

1.9 C. Colorado's Patrick Roy

Bowman directed his comments at Roy in April 1998, after another mêlée erupted in the ongoing blood feud between Detroit and the Colorado Avalanche. This time the mayhem began when Colorado tough guys Jeff Odgers and Warren Rychel took on, among others, the Wings' Kirk Maltby, Martin Lapointe, Bob Rouse and Aaron Ward. With Lapointe on top of the Avs' Tom Fitzgerald, Roy moved in and briefly tried to intervene. Then, Roy focussed his attention on centre ice and challenged Chris Osgood, who had left his crease and dropped his gloves. Osgood, two inches shorter and 15 pounds lighter than Roy, seemed reluctant at first, but the dare had been made. After the two duked it out, the fight ended with a pileup in front of the Detroit bench with Osgood on top of Roy. The next day Bowman admonished Roy, stating that he was "kind of glad he (Roy) didn't win the Olympic medal because we wouldn't have heard the end of it." To which Roy shot back, "Isn't he a Canadian? I wonder what [Brendan] Shanahan and [Steve] Yzerman are thinking right now." Each side, including Osgood's mom, declared its man the victor in the goalie battle. The Detroit goalie left the ice to the chant of "Ozz-ie, Ozz-ie."

1.10 C. New York's A Line

The first hockey triumvirate to earn a nickname that stuck was the Rangers' A Line: Frank Boucher and brothers Bill and Bun

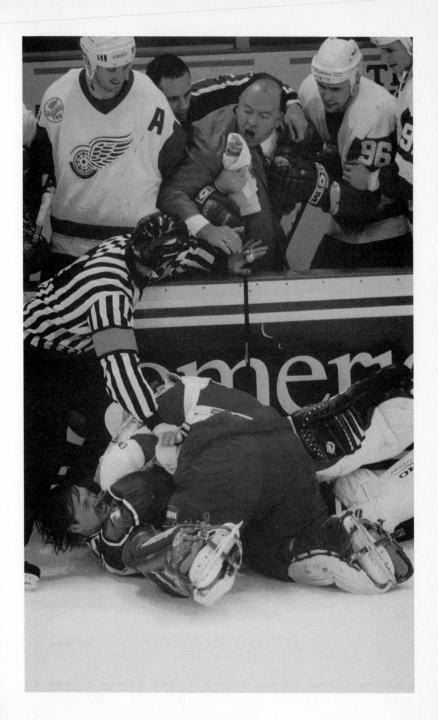

Cook. The Cooks and Boucher are credited with inventing the drop pass, an offensive weapon they executed to perfection in two Stanley Cups for New York in 1928 and 1933. The trio was named after the Eighth Avenue subway line, the A Train, which was built along Eighth Avenue beneath the old Madison Square Garden. The A Line played together from 1926-27 to 1935-36.

1.11 B. A goalie equipment inspector

"Dr. Calipers" is none other than former NHL goalie Dave Dryden (brother of Ken Dryden), the league's watchdog of goaltending equipment standards. Armed with a briefcase of measuring devices, Dryden monitors pads, pants, blockers and sweaters. Any goalie caught cheating is suspended for one game; the offender's team is fined $100,000. Dryden usually measures on game day. However, he is sensitive to how his visits may psyche out goalies, so he works in the afternoon after everyone has left practice. "Everyone's still a little uptight about it . . . (but) everyone's been totally co-operative," said Dryden in a *Dallas Morning News* story. Nobody, from the goalie to the equipment manager to the manufacturers, "want to get caught and have their reputation tarnished."

1.12 D. More than $300,000

Deducted from his $14-million paycheck in 1998-99, Fedorov lost $386,178 thanks to his five-game suspension for a slashing incident in February 1999. Fedorov had swung his stick with his right hand and struck the Islanders' Zdeno Chara on the neck. Chara collapsed and remained on the ice for several minutes. Fedorov was also assessed a match penalty for deliberately injuring a player.

1.13 B. The 1951 death of Toronto's Bill Barilko

Shouts of "Barilko!" became the ritual whenever the Tragically Hip played Maple Leaf Gardens. It was a chant for "Fifty-Mission Cap," a rock hymn about rugged Leaf defenseman Bill Barilko, who, just weeks after scoring a spectacular goal to win the 1951 Stanley Cup, vanished while on a fishing trip in northern Ontario. His Cup winner is considered MLG's most famous goal. To add to the tragedy and mystery of Barilko's disappearance, his downed plane wasn't found for another 12 years. Contrary to most present-day accounts, the discovery of Barilko's plane was not in 1962 but in 1963, just weeks after the Leafs clinched their second Stanley Cup since the accident. Apparently, the plane had run short of fuel but was still on course—half way between Rupert House and Timmins. Barilko's No. 5 has never been worn by another Toronto player.

1.14 D. Paul Laus

NHL players have been fighting since the league's inaugural season in 1917-18. Unfortunately, figures are not available for prior to the 1953-54 season, when the NHL began to keep statistics, but since then the league's leading pugilists have gone from four or five fights in a 70-game schedule to six times that amount during the 1990s. For example, NHL hardrock John Ferguson shared the lead (with Reggie Fleming) with eight fighting majors in 1966-67. Today, heavyweight battlers such as Paul Laus customarily rack up 30 or more fights in a season.

The Baddest Boys of Hockey*

Player	Team	Season	Fighting Majors
Paul Laus	Florida	1996-97	39
Joey Kocur	Detroit	1985-86	36
Jay Miller	Boston	1987-88	34
Mike Peluso	Chicago	1991-92	34
Marc Potvin	LA/Hartford	1993-94	34
Krzysztof Oliwa	New Jersey	1997-98	33
Alan May	Washington	1989-90	32

Current to 1998-99

1.15 C. Eight players

Considering how superstitious most athletes are, you can imagine how popular unlucky No. 13 is among NHLers. Only three players in the history of the Chicago Blackhawks and the Detroit Red Wings, for example, have ever worn No. 13 across their backs. The 80-year-old Montreal Canadiens have never even issued a No. 13. Yet, while most NHLers avoid it, in 1998-99 eight players, mostly Europeans, donned the No. 13: Russians Valeri Kamensky, Slava Kozlov and Andrei Nikolishin; the Czech Republic's Pavel Kubina and Vaclav Prospal; Mats Sundin of Sweden; American Jon Battaglia; and Canadian Claude Lapointe.

1.16 C. Tie Domi
Domi has never had any illusions about why he's in the NHL; he's a fighter, paid to protect the finesse players. Unlike his fellow goons, however, Domi's swagger matches his pugilistic skills. That combination has earned him steady employment, a top-end $1.35-million salary with Toronto and recognition as one of the league's most popular players. Domi, of Albanian ancestry, has done as much as anyone to champion a good fight. As long as the Assassin is around the NHL, there will always be a place in hockey for the big-time duke-out.

1.17 A. Sweden's Borje Salming
Very few players from outside North America have gained entry into the Hockey Hall of Fame. It wasn't until 1989 that Vladislav Tretiak became the first European star elected to the Hall of Fame. However, Tretiak never played in the NHL, so the honour belongs to Salming, the six-time All-Star defenseman with Toronto, who, in 1996, became the Hall's first European-trained NHLer. Two years later, in 1998, Peter Stastny was inducted in his first year of eligibility.

1.18 B. 6.12 goals per game
During the 80-year span between 1917-18 and 1997-98, NHL players averaged slightly more than six goals per game. More recently, 1981-82 produced the highest average (eight goals per game—8.02) when the Edmonton Oilers became the first team in league history to record more than 400 goals in a season. Goal scorers in 1997-98 netted the lowest modern-day average in 42 years (since 1955-56's average of 5.07), scoring only 5.28 goals per game. The highest seasonal average of all time is 9.50

goals in 1917-18, the NHL's first year; the lowest is the paltry 2.92 mark in 1928-29.

1.19 D. A two-game suspension

After beaning a heckling fan with a water bottle November 12, 1998, Simpson was handed a two-game suspension by NHL disciplinarian Colin Campbell. TV cameras caught the Chicago defenseman tossing the plastic bottle at a spectator, near the penalty box in the United Center. "He was mocking Probie (Bob Probert) a bit," Simpson said. "I think everyone is a bit frustrated right now. I just kind of lost my composure." The Hawks were winless in nine games at the time.

1.20 A. Bobby Orr

The first NHLers to break the 100-point mark were Phil Esposito, Bobby Hull and Gordie Howe in 1968-69, all with less than 100 penalty minutes. In the following season, Orr set a number of NHL firsts, including becoming the first defenseman to lead the league in scoring and the first player to notch a 100-point 100-penalty-minute season. Orr recorded 120 points and 125 minutes in box time in 1969-70.

1.21 A. Sweden's Fredrik Olausson

Unlike fellow Swedish blueliner Borje Salming, Olausson has gone largely unnoticed throughout much of his career; few would recognize him, even in his native Sweden. Yet, while Olausson lacks Salming's on-ice charisma, he has made up for it in offensive confidence and staying power. When he scored his 500th NHL point on February 6, 1999, he was in his 13th NHL season. As of 1998-99, Olausson is only the second defenseman born outside North America with a 500-point career, and one of only 36 other rearguards in league history to tally as many points.

1.22 B. The Olympic anthem

No national anthem was played when the former Soviet Union hockey team won the gold at the 1992 Olympics—the Olympic anthem was played instead. Only months earlier, the Soviet Union had broken up and the Soviet Olympic committee called its delegation the Unified Team, in recognition of its athletes from the former Soviet republics. The Unified Team players hit the ice without a logo on their jerseys.

1.23 D. More than 200 millionaires
Among the more than 600 NHLers in 1998-99, a total of 244 players were millionaires (up from 1997-98, when 215 NHL players earned seven-figure salaries). While the 1998-99 average yearly salary also jumped from $1.1 million to $1.2 million between seasons, there was considerable disparity between players. Sergei Fedorov earned $14 million in a front-end loaded deal that paid him $2 million in salary and a $12-million bonus. The lowest-paid players included Ottawa's Steve Leach ($97,000) and Anaheim's Dominic Roussel ($160,000). The average team payroll was $29.6 million, up from $26.6 million a year earlier—a 12 per cent increase.

1.24 C. 508 consecutive games
Murray Murdoch of the New York Rangers is considered the league's first ironman forward. In his 11-year career he never missed a game, playing 508 straight games between 1926-27 and 1936-37. Murdoch's playing days began in Winnipeg on long "reachers," the old steel-bladed skates that were open at both ends. When he hit the NHL, tube skates (a steel blade riveted and soldered into a tube attached to the skate boot) were the preferred choice among players. But Murdoch had trouble adjusting to the tubes, so Rangers general manager Lester Patrick allowed him to use his reachers. By the time the league banned the antiquated blades, the left-winger had made the New York team, scoring 10 points in his first season. Murdoch soon mastered the tube skate and played five straight 44-game schedules, followed by six 48-game years, before retiring in 1937. He helped the Rangers win their first Stanley Cup, in 1928.

1.25 B. Bob Probert
Probert made history by scoring the last goal in the last of the Original Six arenas, the 68-year-old Maple Leaf Gardens. The Chicago tough guy notched the Gardens' final marker at 11:02

of the third period in Chicago's 6-2 thumping of Toronto, February 13, 1999. "I've got the puck and it's going to be put on a plaque," said a jubilant Probert. "I'll never forget this moment." The best observation may have come from sportswriter Cam Cole, who said, "Bob Probert has closed a lot of buildings in his career—many of them, alas, saloons." For the record, Chicago's Harold "Mush" March scored the Gardens' first goal in the 1931 opener. Oddly, March was also the first goal scorer at the old Chicago Stadium.

1.26 B. The Conacher family

It didn't happen until 1998, but the Hall of Fame finally had its first family hat trick when Roy, younger brother of Charlie and Lionel, was posthumously honoured in the veterans category. Charlie, the Big Bomber, starred for Toronto in the 1930s on the Kid Line, with Joe Primeau and Busher Jackson. Charlie was inducted into the Hall in 1961. Lionel, the Big Train, mastered hockey, football, wrestling and boxing and was named Canada's athlete of the half-century in 1950; he was a Hall inductee in 1994. Roy played 11 seasons with Boston, Detroit and Chicago. In his rookie season he led the league in goal scoring and followed up with six goals in the 1939 playoffs, including the Stanley Cup winner for Boston. Even though Roy spent four years in the service during World War II he still finished his career with 226 NHL goals, one more than brother Charlie.

1.27 B. An on-ice act of violence

Slew-footing entered the public's lexicon of hockey terms in the late 1990s, after a rash of on-ice incidents and subsequent suspensions gained media attention in 1998-99. In one frightening episode, Ruslan Salei of Anaheim was given a five-game suspension for simultaneously riding Phoenix's Daniel Briere into the boards while taking his feet out from underneath him. Briere went into convulsions and suffered a concussion. Slew-footing—kicking an opponent's skates out and forward while pushing his body backward with an elbow or stick—renders an adversary totally defenseless in a backward free-fall onto the ice. Even though hockey's heavyweights consider it a dirty, loathsome play.

GAME 1

GRETZKY'S OFFICE

Where is Gretzky's office? What's a spin-a-rama? Who are hockey's zebras? In this game, find the correct definition on the right to match the hockey terms on the left.

(Solutions are on page 116)

1. _____ Sin bin	A. The puck
2. _____ Cage	B. Behind the net
3. _____ Brouhaha	C. A fight
4. _____ Bench boss	D. The goalposts
5. _____ Biscuit	E. An on-ice official
6. _____ A box	F. The coach
7. _____ Gretzky's office	G. The player's bench
8. _____ Goon	H. The net
9. _____ Mucker	I. A 360-degree turn
10. _____ Paddle	J. The penalty box
11. _____ Pipes	K. A fighter
12. _____ Riding the pines	L. Upper part of net
13. _____ Spin-a-rama	M. A goalie stick
14. _____ Zebra	N. A grinder
15. _____ Top shelf	O. Defense formation while shorthanded

2

UNITED WE STAND

Glory often goes to the individual record holder, seldom to the club that helped land a player the hardware. For example, in 1976-77, while Guy Lafleur was turning goalies into pretzels for another scoring championship, Montreal was setting what league all-time team record? During Lafleur's blitz the Canadiens gave no quarter to visiting teams on Montreal Forum ice for a record five-month stretch. They went undefeated in 34 home games (28-0-6) between November 1, 1976, to April 2, 1977. In this chapter we check out various team highs, from record-winning streaks to the league's highest ticket prices.

(Answers are on page 23)

2.1 What is the longest winning streak by an NHL team?
   A. 13 consecutive wins
   B. 17 consecutive wins
   C. 21 consecutive wins
   D. 24 consecutive wins

2.2 According to *Forbes* magazine, which NHL franchise was the most valuable in 1997-98?
   A. The New York Rangers
   B. The Detroit Red Wings
   C. The Montreal Canadiens
   D. The Philadelphia Flyers

2.3 Which expansion team in the 1990s recorded the most points in its inaugural season?
   A. The San Jose Sharks in 1991-92
   B. The Florida Panthers in 1993-94
   C. The Anaheim Mighty Ducks in 1993-94
   D. The Nashville Predators in 1998-99

2.4 What is the most number of goalies one team had under contract in one season?
A. Four goalies
B. Six goalies
C. Eight goalies
D. 10 goalies

2.5 When was the NHL's last bench-clearing brawl?
A. The 1960s
B. The 1970s
C. The 1980s
D. The 1990s

2.6 What is the most number of NHL teams for which one player has had a 20-goal season?
A. Four NHL teams
B. Five NHL teams
C. Six NHL teams
D. Seven NHL teams

2.7 For which NHL team was Roger Neilson coaching during the famous Roger Neilson paper bag episode?
A. The Vancouver Canucks
B. The New York Rangers
C. The Philadelphia Flyers
D. The Toronto Maple Leafs

2.8 What is the NHL record for most consecutive ties by a team from the start of a season?
A. Three ties
B. Four ties
C. Five ties
D. Six ties

2.9 What is the name of TV commentator Don Cherry's hockey team in the Ontario Hockey League?
A. The Mississauga IceDogs
B. The Barrie Colts
C. The Ottawa 67s
D. The Brampton Battalion

2.10 Which team besides the Edmonton Oilers of the 1980s can boast four 40-goal scorers in one season?
A. The 1970-71 Boston Bruins
B. The 1979-80 Montreal Canadiens
C. The 1987-88 Calgary Flames
D. The 1995-96 Pittsburgh Penguins

2.11 What is the highest number of penalty minutes amassed by one NHL team in one regular season?
A. Between 1,000 and 2,000 penalty minutes
B. Between 2,000 and 3,000 penalty minutes
C. Between 3,000 and 4,000 penalty minutes
D. More than 4,000 penalty minutes

2.12 Which two NHL clubs are the only teams ever to compete for the Capital Cup?
A. The Detroit Red Wings and the Toronto Maple Leafs
B. The Toronto Maple Leafs and the Montreal Canadiens
C. The Montreal Canadiens and the Ottawa Senators
D. The Ottawa Senators and the Washington Capitals

2.13 Which of these Canadian NHL teams paid the most property taxes in 1998-99?
A. The Montreal Canadiens
B. The Vancouver Canucks
C. The Ottawa Senators
D. The Toronto Maple Leafs

2.14 Which 1970s team featured the Mafia Line?
A. The Detroit Red Wings
B. The Chicago Blackhawks
C. The New York Rangers
D. The Philadelphia Flyers

2.15 What was the average ticket price for the league's 27 teams in 1998-99?
A. Between $25 and $30
B. Between $30 and $35
C. Between $35 and $40
D. More than $40

2.16 Which NHL team of the late 1990s was notoriously poor at scoring shorthanded goals, and failed to record any in more than 100 games?
A. The Montreal Canadiens
B. The New York Rangers
C. The San Jose Sharks
D. The Detroit Red Wings

2.17 How long was the longest uninterrupted road trip made by an NHL team—in league history?
A. 10 days on the road
B. 14 days on the road
C. 18 days on the road
D. 22 days on the road

2.18 What is the record for the longest non-winning streak *on the road* by a team (from the time it entered the NHL) against another team?
A. 25 games
B. 35 games
C. 45 games
D. 55 games

2.19 What is the record for the longest non-winning streak by a team (from the time it entered the NHL) against another team?

A. 14 games
B. 24 games
C. 34 games
D. 44 games

UNITED WE STAND
Answers

2.1 **B. 17 consecutive wins**
The longest winning streak in NHL annals belongs to the 1992-93 Pittsburgh Penguins. After missing 23 games to cancer, Mario Lemieux roared back in top form to lead the Penguins to a record 17 straight wins between March 9 and April 9, 1993. Coached by Scotty Bowman, Pittsburgh surpassed the previous record of 15 consecutive wins set by the New York Islanders in 1981-82. Interestingly, only two teams in the top seven won the Stanley Cup in the year of their streak: the 1981-82 Islanders and the 1967-68 Canadiens.

The NHL's Longest Winning Streaks*		
Team	**Season**	**Length**
Pittsburgh Penguins	1992-93	17 wins
New York Islanders	1981-82	15 wins
Boston Bruins	1929-30	14 wins
Boston Bruins	1970-71	13 wins
Philadelphia Flyers	1985-86	13 wins
Montreal Canadiens	1967-68	12 wins
Colorado Avalanche	1998-99	12 wins
Current to 1998-99		

2.2 **A. The New York Rangers**
The most valuable franchise in North American pro sports is the NFL Dallas Cowboys, worth $413 million. Among hockey teams, the New York Rangers, valued at $195 million, are

number one in the NHL but just 51st overall. The Flyers are second at $187 million; Boston third at $185 million; Detroit fourth at $184 million. The Canadiens were the most valuable Canadian franchise (in 1997-98) at $167 million. Calgary ($76 million) and Edmonton ($67 million) placed 26th and 27th among all NHL teams. (Estimates are based on revenues, expenses and team facilities. All figures are in U.S. dollars.)

2.3 B. The Florida Panthers in 1993-94

Masterminded by Bill Torrey, architect of the New York Islanders dynasty of the 1980s, the first-year Panthers won 33 games and finished with 83 points, a .494 win-loss percentage and the best record among all expansion teams in NHL history. Torrey's front office included manager Bobby Clarke and coach Roger Neilson, two hockey men who stocked their lunchpail team with tough, reliable veterans such as captain Brian Skrudland, Bill Lindsay and Scott Mellanby. Clarke took advantage of favourable draft rules and selected former Rangers star John Vanbiesbrouck and Islanders backup Mark Fitzpatrick to tend goal. The veteran skaters were surrounded by young draft picks, including Rob Niedermayer and the midseason addition of Stu Barnes. The Panthers gelled and became the Cinderella team of 1993-94: they almost made the postseason, missing the final playoff berth by one point.

2.4 C. Eight goalies

It was the kind of crisis no NHL general manager has ever faced before. During the 1998-99 season, Calgary goalies were going down so fast the Flames set a league benchmark, becoming the first team to have eight goalies under contract at the same time. The eighth netminder signed, Fred Brathwaite, was, when he played, the sixth Flames goaltender to get a start and the fourth to backstop Calgary in one 12-day period. So many netminders were stepping into the breach that when Brathwaite walked into the Flames dressing room, his locker name-plate read "Braithwaite" (misspelled with an extra "i"). Then, the public-address announcer at the Saddledome called him *Jeff* Brathwaith. The "Who's on first?" scenario turned into a crisis as Calgary called in backups from the AHL, the IHL, junior and the ECHL (Brathwaith came from the Canadian Olympic team). The collapse began when veteran Ken Wregget went down with a bad back. Then, backup Tyler Moss suffered a groin pull; Jean Giguere, a pulled hamstring; Andrei Trefilov, a shoulder injury. Junior Tyrone Garner played one game, a 5-1 loss to Pittsburgh, before Brathwaite got the call. Two other netminders were on standby: Igor Karpenko of Calgary's AHL affiliate in Saint John, New Brunswick, and free-agent goalie Pavel Nestak of Jonestown in the ECHL. The silver lining for Calgary may have been Brathwaite, who rescued his career from minor-league obscurity and earned a 1.65 goals-against average and a .947 save percentage after seven consecutive starts.

2.5   C. The 1980s

Until anti-brawling legislation was introduced during the late 1970s and beefed up in the early 1980s, bench-clearing battles were relatively common in hockey (there were sometimes five or six incidents per year). But the third-man-in rule, game misconducts and heavy fines (levied against anyone intervening in an altercation or anyone who didn't go to the bench area during a fight) soon eliminated bench-clearing brawls. The last full-scale mêlée was on February 26, 1987, when the Quebec Nordiques and the Boston Bruins emptied both benches in a battle that led to nine ejections and 167 penalty minutes. Ironically, the fight came one night after Boston city council rejected a proposed ordinance allowing city police to arrest athletes in the middle of a game for assault. (Later, on May 14, 1987, another all-out brawl occurred between Montreal and Philadelphia, but that was a pregame situation that erupted over players' superstitions during the warmup skate.)

2.6   C. Six NHL teams

Right-winger Ray Sheppard has notched 20 goals or more with every team he's played on in the NHL. Prior to February 22, 1999, when he scored his 20th with the Carolina Hurricanes, Sheppard recorded 20-goal years with Buffalo, Detroit, San Jose, Florida and the New York Rangers.

2.7   D. The Toronto Maple Leafs

Maple Leaf owner Harold Ballard can take credit for many fiascoes in his time, but few debacles compare to the outrageousness of the Roger Neilson paper bag episode. After the club fell below .500 in February 1979, Ballard promised a TV audience that he would fire Neilson if the Leafs lost their next game. True to his word and blind in his arrogance, Ballard, after Toronto bowed to Montreal, impetuously fired Neilson—again on TV. Unfortunately for the Leafs, Ballard had no replacement in mind. And after scout Gerry McNamara and AHL coach Eddie Johnston turned down his offers, the Leaf owner was forced to rehire Neilson. To save face and make it appear as if it was all a well-concocted hoax, Ballard instructed Neilson—through Gregory—to appear behind the bench at the start of the next game wearing a paper bag over his head. At an appropriate dramatic moment, after the national anthem, Neilson was to come out and rip the bag off his head to reveal to the expectant Maple Leaf Gardens crowd that the next coach of Toronto was Neilson himself. As Toronto captain Darryl Sittler said in a *National Post* story, "I remember we were waiting to go on the ice for the start of the game, and Harold was standing at the dressing room door with the paper bag. As Roger walked by, Harold said, 'C'mon, c'mon, put it on.'" Neilson refused and strode by Ballard to take his position behind the bench. The Leafs won the game, but at the end of that season Neilson was fired.

2.8   B. Four ties

In 1997-98 the New York Rangers became the first team in NHL history to start the season with four ties, tying the Islanders 2-2 (October 3) in the season opener, Los Angeles 2-2 (October 5), Edmonton 3-3 (October 8) and Calgary 1-1 (October 9). The Rangers' "tie" streak ended October 11, when they played Vancouver in their first game since Mark Messier was signed away from New York by the Canucks. Messier scored a goal against his former teammates, but Rangers captain and former Messier teammate Wayne Gretzky notched a hat trick in the 6-3 New York win.

2.9   A. The Mississauga IceDogs

In their first OHL season, Cherry's IceDogs came to the rink with more bark than bite. As the toughest team in the OHL they were also the worst. The IceDogs established a new league-low with a 4-61-3 record. They led the league in penalties and scored only 145 goals, breaking the previous CHL record for futility: 154 by the Toronto St. Michael's Majors. Numerous problems beset Cherry's team. First, in keeping with the hockey principals of their master, the IceDogs boycotted European players. Also, the OHL draft that year wasn't favourable to expansion teams. With the club's losses piling up, most players suffered emotionally as they forgot what winning felt like. The IceDogs' worst defeats came a week apart in February 1999: a 15-0 humiliation at the hands of the Barrie Colts, followed by a 13-0 hammering by the Ottawa 67s.

2.10   C. The 1987-88 Calgary Flames

Besides the Edmonton Oilers, only one other NHL team has managed to feature four 40-goal scorers in one year: the 1987-88 Flames. Calgary rookie Joe Nieuwendyk scored 51 goals; Hakan Loob, 50; Mike Bullard, 48; and Joe Mullen, 40. The power-house Oilers did it four consecutive times during the 1980s.

Most 40-or-More-Goal Scorers in One Year*		
Team	**Year**	**Players**
Edmonton	1982-83	W. Gretzky (71), G. Anderson (48), M. Messier (48), J. Kurri (45)
Edmonton	1983-84	W. Gretzky (87), G. Anderson (54), J. Kurri (52), P. Coffey (40)
Edmonton	1984-85	W. Gretzky (73), J. Kurri (71), M. Krushelnyski (43), G. Anderson (42)
Edmonton	1985-86	J. Kurri (68), G. Anderson (54), W. Gretzky (52), P. Coffey (48)
Calgary	1987-88	J. Nieuwendyk (51), H. Loob (50), M. Bullard (48), J. Mullen (40)

Current to 1998-99

2.11 B. Between 2,000 and 3,000 penalty minutes

No NHL team has amassed more box time in one season than the 1991-92 Buffalo Sabres—a record 2,713 penalty minutes. Leading the assault were Rob Ray with 354 minutes and Gord Donnelly and Brad May with 309 each. The three Sabres tough guys accumulated almost 1,000 minutes among them. Combined, they averaged 34 penalty minutes per game!

2.12 D. The Ottawa Senators and the Washington Capitals

The Capital Cup was purchased in 1992 by Ottawa Senators founder Bruce Firestone, as a publicity gimmick to hype his struggling team. The concept was an annual two-game exhibition series between the two respective national capitals. But the Senators-Capitals rivalry died without much notice after Ottawa failed to present any real competitive threat. Washington's name appears on the Cup four successive years, though former Senators general manager Randy Sexton claims Ottawa won one series. The crystalline mug's current resting place is a Senators storage room.

2.13 A. The Montreal Canadiens

One of the biggest issues facing Canadian NHL teams for the last decade has been government tax subsidies. The situation has grown so tenuous that Canadian clubs believe they are being taxed into extinction. The disparity with American teams is sobering. While U.S. teams receive massive tax breaks and free arenas paid for by municipal and state governments, teams in Canada pay dearly for buildings, infrastructure and real estate. In 1996-97, the 20 American NHL teams spent a combined total of $2.2 million in property taxes. In comparison, the six Canadian teams paid almost 10 times the U.S figure, or $21.8 million. The big hurt is felt most in Montreal, where the Canadiens fork over the largest single portion, a league-high $11 million in taxes. That's more than half of what the other five Canadian NHL teams pay combined, or just a few million dollars less than the entire league's payout. As of this writing, the Habs are fighting the property bill in court, and Toronto may face taxes of $14 million at the new Air Canada Centre. (All figures are in Canadian dollars.)

2.14 C. The New York Rangers
During the 1978-79 season, the Rangers were led by the Mafia Line of "Godfather" Phil Esposito (left wing) and his two dons—Don Murdoch (centre) and rookie Don Maloney (right wing). Murdoch might never have played on the infamous New York line if his year-long suspension for cocaine possession had not been commuted to 40 games. Maloney scored 20 points in the playoffs that year, setting an NHL record by a rookie.

2.15 D. More than $40
Among the four major team sports in North America, hockey's average ticket price of $42.79 ranks a close second behind the National Football League ($42.86/ticket), but is more expensive than the National Basketball Association ($36.32/ticket) and Major League Baseball ($13.60/ticket). The highest ticket average is at MSG, for the Rangers ($58.83/ticket); the lowest tickets are at the Saddledome, for the Flames ($26.04/ticket). (All figures are in U.S. dollars.)

2.16 B. The New York Rangers
New York's infamous stretch of games without a shorthanded goal lasted for 121 games: from the final match of the 1996-97 season (when Mark Messier left town) until January 10, 1999. The streak, considered the longest by a wide margin, was snapped by John MacLean's penalty-shot goal against Tampa Bay's Bill Ranford.

2.17 C. 18 days on the road
It's the unofficial record for the longest stretch of away games in league history; or as San Jose Sharks assistant coach Bernie Nicholls put it, it was "the road trip from hell." For 18 days, from February 3 to 21, 1999, the Sharks lived out of a suitcase and played 10 road games in nine cities over four time zones. San Jose travelled from the dry heat of Phoenix on the west coast to the deep freeze of Chicago, then on to balmy Florida and Washington, north for more cold weather in Detroit and finally home to the warmth of San Jose. Only the Calgary Flames played a longer string of road games—11 in 1987-88

during the Winter Olympics in Calgary—but they returned home for the NHL All-Star break after three games. The Sharks' 10-game exile from San Jose Arena was partially self-inflicted; the franchise leased the building to a tennis tournament and the *Disney on Ice* show during February. The Sharks completed the gruelling road trip with a 4-5-1 record, closing with three straight defeats to Detroit, Buffalo and Washington. Those losses ruined San Jose's chances to become the first team to finish better than .500 on a road trip of nine or more games.

2.18 B. 35 games
The worst on-the-road non-win record by a team is owned by the Minnesota North Stars, who couldn't win or tie a game against the Bruins at Boston Gardens in 35 road games. The North Stars managed their first win in seven years on November 8, 1981, after posting a 0-28-7 record against Boston. Two other teams needed seven seasons to beat their rivals on the road: the Kansas City-Colorado-New Jersey franchise went through three different cities and 26 games (0-24-2) before scoring a victory against the Islanders at Long Island on December 11, 1984; Washington played 23 winless games (0-22-1) against the Montreal Canadiens at the Forum before the team's first triumph on November 26, 1983.

2.19 C. 34 games
In what is considered the longest non-winning streak between teams, the Washington Capitals failed to record a victory against the Montreal Canadiens in almost six years—from 1974-75, their first NHL season, until February 19, 1980. The Caps played in 31 losses and three ties before notching their first victory against Montreal, a 3-1 win at the Capital Center. Not mincing words, Caps captain Ryan Walter said, "We had a barrier about not beating Montreal." The winless streak ended after Bengt Gustaffson scored the go-ahead goal and Mike Gardiner potted an empty netter. Goalie Wayne Stephenson earned the Washington win. Overall, the once anemic Capitals own the top three of four spots in this category, falling short 26 consecutive times against Boston and 19 times against the

Islanders. As of 1998-99, the longest drought by an expansion team belongs to the San Jose Sharks, who haven't beaten the Rangers since entering the league in 1991—seven frustrating seasons with a 0-13-2 record against New York.

The NHL's Longest Winless Streaks*		
Team vs. Team	**Record**	**Ended**
Washington vs. Montreal	0-31-3	Feb. 19, 1980
Washington vs. Boston	0-21-5	March 12, 1980
Ottawa vs. Boston	0-20-2	Jan. 1, 1997
Washington vs. Islanders	0-16-3	April 1, 1979
Islanders vs. Buffalo	0-12-5	Dec. 7, 1975
San Jose vs. Rangers	0-13-2	—
KC-Col vs. Philadelphia	0-13-0	Jan. 28, 1978
KC-Col vs. Buffalo	0-11-2	Dec. 13, 1977
Current to 1998-99/Courtesy of the National Post		

GAME 2

THE AGE OF EXPANSION

At no time in the history of the NHL did league expansion occur so rapidly as in the 1990s. In 10 seasons, 13 franchises came into the fold as either new or transferred teams. NHL clubs sprang up in sunbelt cities such as Dallas and Tampa Bay or moved from Winnipeg to Phoenix. In this game, all 13 team names and host cities appear in the puzzle horizontally, vertically or backwards. Some are easily found, such as NASHVILLE; others require a more careful search. After you've circled all the team and city names, read the remaining 29 letters in descending order to spell our hidden phrase.

(Solutions are on page 116)

N	A	N	I	L	O	R	A	C	E	A	T	M	I
F	L	O	R	I	D	A	P	H	O	E	N	I	X
H	S	E	T	O	Y	O	C	O	N	A	A	G	M
D	U	C	K	S	E	N	A	T	O	R	S	H	I
Y	P	R	E	D	A	T	O	R	S	T	H	T	N
A	A	L	R	L	W	T	H	O	E	D	V	Y	N
B	T	O	A	I	T	C	D	K	S	A	I	T	E
A	L	V	L	A	C	A	C	A	O	L	L	H	S
P	A	D	W	K	R	A	N	E	J	L	L	R	O
M	N	A	Y	O	J	A	N	L	N	A	E	A	T
A	T	E	L	E	H	A	G	E	A	S	U	S	A
T	A	O	U	E	S	R	A	T	S	E	E	H	X
P	C	L	I	G	H	T	N	I	N	G	A	E	N
S	B	M	I	P	A	N	T	H	E	R	S	R	O
N	S	K	R	A	H	S	U	B	M	U	L	O	C

3

THE CREASE KINGS

One of hockey's most remarkable goalie tandems came together in 1968-69, when aging veterans Jacques Plante and Glenn Hall teamed up for the St. Louis Blues and won the Vezina Trophy with the league's lowest goals-against average. Plante, 40, had been lured out of retirement and coupled with Hall, 37, another demigod netminder from the six-team era; they combined to produce the best season average by a whopping 39-goal margin. During the 76-game schedule, Hall and Plante allowed only 157 goals. To this day, Plante is the oldest netminder to win the Vezina, the game's most important goalie award.

(Answers are on page 37)

3.1   If a team plays two goalies in a win, who is always credited with the victory?
   A. The goalie who started the game
   B. The goalie who plays the most minutes in the game
   C. The goalie who is on the ice for the game winner
   D. The goalie who finished the game

3.2   Which goalie earned the last wins at both the Montreal Forum and Maple Leaf Gardens?
   A. Curtis Joseph
   B. Jocelyn Thibault
   C. Felix Potvin
   D. Patrick Roy

3.3   Which famous old-time goalie was known as the "Chicoutimi Cucumber"?
   A. Chuck Gardiner
   B. George Hainsworth
   C. Alex Connell
   D. Georges Vezina

3.4 In what decade was the first Crouch Collar invented?
A. The 1950s
B. The 1960s
C. The 1970s
D. The 1980s

3.5 Since the Hart Trophy (league MVP) was first awarded in 1924, how many goalies have won it?
A. Five goalies
B. 10 goalies
C. 15 goalies
D. 20 goalies

3.6 Which goalie was the last active NHLer who played in the WHA's inaugural season?
A. Mike Liut
B. Joe Daley
C. Richard Brodeur
D. Bernie Parent

3.7 Who is the only goalie since expansion in 1967 to allow three five-goal games by one player in one season?
A. Mike Liut
B. Pete Peeters
C. Grant Fuhr
D. Jon Casey

3.8 What is the most number of consecutive games that one NHL team has allowed two goals or less? Name the goalie.
A. Eight straight games
B. 18 straight games
C. 28 straight games
D. 38 straight games

3.9 Which two goalies in 1998-99 set the post-expansion NHL record for allowing two goals or less in most consecutive games?
A. Buffalo's Dominik Hasek and Dwayne Roloson
B. Philadelphia's John Vanbiesbrouck and Ron Hextall
C. New Jersey's Martin Brodeur and Chris Terreri
D. Phoenix's Jimmy Waite and Nikolai Khabibulin

3.10 How many NHL goalies are 20-year men?
A. Only one goalie, Terry Sawchuk
B. Two goalies
C. Four goalies
D. Six goalies

3.11 As of 1998-99, what is the most number of 40-game seasons played by an NHL goalie?
A. 10
B. 12
C. 14
D. 16

3.12 Which NHL goalie recorded the most double-digit shutout seasons in league history?
A. Alex Connell
B. Tiny Thompson
C. Terry Sawchuk
D. Bernie Parent

3.13 As of 1998-99, which European-born goalie has played in the most NHL games?
A. Sweden's Tommy Salo
B. The Czech Republic's Dominik Hasek
C. Latvia's Arturs Irbe
D. Poland's Peter Sidorkiewicz

3.14 During the 1990s, how many different NHL netminders posted goals-against averages below 2.00?
A. Only one goalie, Dominik Hasek
B. Three goalies
C. Five goalies
D. Seven goalies

3.15 Which old-time goaltender allowed the first five-goal game by an NHL forward?
A. Harry Holmes
B. Clint Benedict
C. John Roach
D. Georges Vezina

3.16 Which goalie played the most games with one team?
A. Tony Esposito of the Chicago Blackhawks
B. Terry Sawchuk of the Detroit Red Wings
C. Glenn Hall of the Chicago Blackhawks
D. Billy Smith of the New York Islanders

3.17 Which goalie played the most 70-game seasons?
A. Glenn Hall
B. Terry Sawchuk
C. Grant Fuhr
D. Ed Belfour

3.18 What is the greatest number of tied games recorded by a goalie in a career?
A. Between 50 and 100 games
B. Between 100 and 150 games
C. Between 150 and 200 games
D. More than 200 games

3.19 Why was old-time goalie Cecil Thompson nicknamed "Tiny"?
A. Because of his small size
B. Because of his low goals-against average
C. Because of his large size
D. Because of his undersize goalie pads

3.20 What is the greatest number of goals scored against Dominik Hasek in a regular-season game?

A. Six goals against

B. Seven goals against

C. Eight goals against

D. Nine goals against

3.21 What is the oldest age of an NHL goals-against-average leader?

A. 30 years old

B. 34 years old

C. 38 years old

D. 42 years old

THE CREASE KINGS
Answers

3.1 **C. The goalie who is on the ice for the game winner**

Even though a netminder may play most of a game (including the start and finish), he is not credited with the win unless he is *on the ice* for the game winner. That technicality has twice prevented Patrick Roy from victories. On the second occasion, December 21, 1998, Roy lost career victory number 391 after he was pulled in the second period to give Colorado's weary power-play unit a few extra seconds of rest. With the score tied 2-2 and a two-man advantage on the Mighty Ducks, Avalanche coach Bob Hartley replaced Roy with Craig Billington. Colorado rookie Milan Hejduk scored what proved to be the game winner, and even though he didn't face a single shot and returned to the bench, Billington got the win because he was on the ice for it. Roy played 58:08; Billington, 1:52. Fair? No way! After the game Roy's displeasure was obvious. He stated, sarcastically, that Hartley made a "great" decision, then, to get his point across, he used his stick to trash some video equipment in Hartley's office.

3.2 B. Jocelyn Thibault

More than 130 years of hockey were played at Maple Leaf Gardens and the Montreal Forum, but the last games in both old barns were won by the same netminder: Jocelyn Thibault. Backstopping the Canadiens, Thibault defeated Dallas 4-1 March 11, 1996, in the Forum's finale. Then, almost three years later (as a Blackhawk), T-Bo humbled Toronto 6-2, February 13, 1999, in the last match at MLG. "I'm a pretty historic goalie," laughed Thibault after realizing he was 2-0 in arena closings. That night at the Gardens, Thibault, 24, joined an elite group of goaltenders for another reason. He notched his 100th career NHL victory. (Only four other active goalies had won 100 games so early in their careers: Martin Brodeur, Patrick Roy, Grant Fuhr and Tom Barrasso.)

3.3 D. Georges Vezina

Georges Vezina, after which the Vezina Trophy is named, became known as the Chicoutimi Cucumber for his capacity to stay cool under pressure. Born in Chicoutimi, Quebec, Vezina joined the Montreal Canadiens in 1910-11 and never missed a regular season or playoff game over the next 15 years. His 367-game streak ended in November 1925 when chest pains forced him to the bench. Four months later he died of tuberculosis; the Canadiens donated the Vezina Trophy to honour his memory and the best NHL goalie in future seasons. Vezina was one of two goalies (Chuck Gardiner was the other) first elected to the Hockey Hall of Fame in 1945.

3.4 C. The 1970s

The Crouch Collar dates to 1975 when Kim Crouch, an 18-year-old goalie in the Ontario Junior A league, nearly bled to death on-ice after a skateblade severed his jugular vein. The six-inch gash in Crouch's neck took 40 stitches to close. Motivated by the near fatal accident, Crouch's father, Ed, a firefighter in Whitby, Ontario, invented the Crouch Collar. Made of ballistic nylon, the one-and-a-half-inch-high collar has a small protective bib that covers the area just below the neck. The first model was patented in Canada in 1976.

3.5 A. Five goalies

In almost 75 years of Hart Trophy winners only five goalies have been named regular-season league MVP. Curiously, almost without exception, each of the award-winning goalies played on mediocre teams. Much like Dominik Hasek's influence on the very average Buffalo Sabres, the previous Hart recipients inspired their teams to levels of confidence far greater than the sum of their talent alone. The first goalie MVP was New York's Roy Worters, who led the anemic Americans to a second-place finish in 1929. In 1950, the Rangers' Chuck Rayner earned Hart status and New York a playoff spot with a team that had no player finishing better than 17th in the scoring race. Despite the Blackhawks' last-place finish in 1954, Al Rollins gave Chicago some respectability through a dismal season of 12-51-7. Montreal's Jacques Plante might be the exception among Hart-winning goalies. He took the faltering but talent-rich Canadiens, a club whose best scorer that season was third-line centre Ralph Backstrom, to first overall with a 13-point edge over second-place Toronto in 1962. The fifth Hart-winning goalie is Hasek, the only goalie to claim the prestigious award twice, with back-to-back wins in 1997 and 1998. In both seasons, Hasek, backstopping the middle-of-the-pack Sabres, led the league with save percentages of .930 and .932.

3.6 C. Richard Brodeur

Before his stint as King Richard in Vancouver, Brodeur backstopped the old Quebec Nordiques of the WHA. He signed with Quebec right out of junior hockey in 1972, the WHA's first season, and became one of the rival league's best goalies. In seven WHA seasons Brodeur posted 165 WHA victories—second in all-time wins to Winnipeg goalie Joe Daley's 167. Brodeur led the Nordiques to the Avco Cup championship in 1977 and Vancouver to the Stanley Cup finals in 1982. Brodeur retired in 1988, the last active NHLer who played in the WHA's inaugural season.

3.7 B. Pete Peeters

Between 1967-68 and 1998-99 only two goalies, Mike Liut and Pete Peeters, have been scored upon five times by one player three times in their careers. Only Peeters managed it in one season, 1981-82. The Philadelphia netminder surrendered four goals to Edmonton's Wayne Gretzky and the empty net-ter—Gretzky's historic 50th in 39 games—(December 30); five goals to Bryan Trottier of the New York Islanders (February 13); and five goals to Winnipeg's Willy Lindstrom (March 2). In NHL history only two other goalies have been disgraced by three five-goal games. Clint Benedict recorded a trio in his career and Howard Lockhart, like Peeters, suffered through three with the Hamilton Tigers in 1920-21. In a six-week period, Lockhart was humiliated 10-3, 12-5 and 10-5 in NHL games. Despite his 5.45 goals-against average that year, Lockhart played another full season in Hamilton and brought his numbers down to 4.39. At least he didn't suffer another five-goal game.

3.8 B. 18 straight games

Fronted by perhaps the era's best defensive duo in the NHL—Norris Trophy-winners Doug Harvey and Tom Johnson—Montreal's Jacques Plante allowed two goals or less for a record 18 games in 1959-60. The streak began on October 22 and ended in Game 19 after a 7-4 loss to the Rangers December 3. Plante's record was 14-1-3. Ironically, after all the criticism Plante faced over the use of his goalie mask, it was during this period that he became hockey's first masked netminder.

3.9 D. Phoenix's Jimmy Waite and Nikolai Khabibulin

The Coyotes got off to their best start in franchise history with a 14-3-2 record in their first 19 games of 1998-99. During that span Phoenix established a post-expansion NHL record of allowing two goals or less in 17 consecutive games, leaving them just one shy of the all-time 18-game record set by the Montreal Canadiens in 1959-60. In their season opener October 11 the Coyotes lost 4-1 to Ottawa, but didn't allow more than two goals in the next 17 games until their 4-3 loss to Edmonton on December 2. Many factors contributed to their long run, including the leadership of Keith Tkachuk and Jeremy Roenick, free-agent signings such as Greg Adams and Rick Tocchet, plus the league's best penalty-killing unit and the rock-solid play of Khabibulin and Waite, who combined for a stellar 1.51 GAA during the drive.

3.10 B. Two goalies
The NHL hasn't seen a 20-year backstopper since Terry Sawchuk and Gump Worsley retired in the 1970s after each played for 21 seasons. Sawchuk stopped pucks over four decades from 1949-50 to 1969-70; Worsley, from 1952-53 to 1973-74. Currently, only a handful of netminders have managed 15-year-or-more careers, including Grant Fuhr and John Vanbiesbrouck.

3.11 C. 14
In 1998-99, two goalies—John Vanbiesbrouck and Patrick Roy—became the first netminders in NHL history to record 14 40-game seasons, surpassing the benchmarks of Glenn Hall, Gilles Meloche and Tony Esposito, each with 13 40-game seasons. Tom Barrasso trails with 13 40-game seasons.

3.12 C. Terry Sawchuk
Sawchuk didn't become the NHL's shutout king without nailing a few double-digit shutout seasons. During his 21-year Hall of Fame career, Sawchuk had four seasons of 10 or more shutouts, beginning in 1950-51 (11 shutouts), followed by 1951-52 (12 shutouts), 1953-54 (12 shutouts) and 1954-55 (12 shutouts). Few modern-day goalies have approached Sawchuk's mark. Other goalies, including Alex Connell, Lorne Chabot and Tiny Thompson, all recorded three double-digit seasons, but did so prior to 1929-30 when forward passing was illegal and the game was more defensive in nature.

3.13 B. The Czech Republic's Dominik Hasek
As of 1998-99, Hasek played in 414 NHL matches, the most games by any European-born goalie. But even before he established his credentials as the Dominator in North America, Hasek ruled without challengers. In his native Czechoslovakia, he was named goaltender of the year five years in a row between 1985-86 and 1989-90. Once in the NHL, his track to stardom was soon established. In 1993-94 he recorded a 1.95 GAA, the

first below-2.00 average since Bernie Parent's 1.89 mark in 1973-74. Later, he won back-to-back Hart Trophies as league MVP in 1997 and 1998, an NHL first by a goaltender. His reputation as a world goalie was cemented at the 1998 Olympics when he led the Czech Republic to a surprising gold medal by upsetting all favourites at the tournament, including Canada, the United States and Russia.

3.14 C. Five goalies

Despite tinkering with the rules to boost scoring in the NHL, goaltenders racked up even more impressive numbers with each successive season during the 1990s. With or without the help of sophisticated neutral-zone traps and obstruction techniques, it was the great goalie era. Arguably, it began with Patrick Roy, when he led the Montreal Canadiens to surprise Stanley Cups in 1986 and 1993. The following season, Dominik Hasek recorded a 1.95 goals-against average, becoming the first below-2.00 goalie since Philadelphia's Bernie Parent 20 years earlier. Then, Martin Brodeur, a Roy prodigy, recorded back-to-back seasons of 1.88 and 1.89 in 1996-97 and 1997-98. It marked the first year since Terry Sawchuk and Harry Lumley each had consecutive averages below 2.00 (in 1953-54 and 1954-55). Another mark was equalled in 1997-98 when Ed Belfour earned a 1.88 average, the first time two goalies (Belfour and Brodeur) notched below-2.00 averages in 43 years. In 1998-99, goaltenders earned even better results. At no time since the early 1930s have more than two netminders scored below-2.00 averages in one season. In 1998-99, an unprecedented four goalies all scored better than 2.00: Ron Tugnutt (1.79), Dominik Hasek (1.87), Byron Dafoe (1.99) and Ed Belfour (1.99). In all, five starting goalies during the 1990s recorded below-2.00 averages. They were Dominik Hasek, Martin Brodeur, Ed Belfour, Byron Dafoe and Ron Tugnutt.

3.15 B. Clint Benedict

The great Joe Malone scored the NHL's first five-goal game in a 7-4 win over Clint Benedict and the Ottawa Senators on December 19, 1917, the first night the league began operations.

3.16 A. Tony Esposito of the Chicago Blackhawks

Even though Sawchuk's 971 career games total is an NHL record among goalies, Esposito spent the most time with one team. Tony O's skill and durability kept him active from 1968-69 to 1983-84 in 886 regular-season games; all but his first 13 matches (in Montreal) were with Chicago.

Most Games Played with One Team*

Goalie	Team	GP
Tony Esposito	Chicago	873
Terry Sawchuk	Detroit	734
Billy Smith	NYI	675
Glenn Hall	Chicago	618
Gump Worsley	NYR	583
Jacques Plante	Montreal	556
Patrick Roy	Montreal	551

Current to 1999

3.17 A. Glenn Hall

During his never-to-be-broken ironman streak of 551 games between 1956-57 and 1962-63, Hall played an amazing seven straight seasons of 70 games for Detroit and Chicago. No other NHL goalie has ever come close to Hall's mark. Belfour, Fuhr and Sawchuk each have the next-highest marks: three 70-game seasons.

3.18 C. Between 150 and 200 games

Old-time goalie Terry Sawchuk still holds many NHL records, including most tied games. Sawchuk knotted 188 games in his 21-year career, compared to Glenn Hall (165), Tony Esposito (151) and Gump Worsley (150), netminders with the next most career ties. The top active goalie is Grant Fuhr, who, as of 1998-99, had 112 tied games to his credit.

3.19 B. Because of his low goals-against average

Thompson's nickname, "Tiny," came about because of the minuscule size of his goals-against average, not because of his height or weight. (In his era, Tiny was actually considered big at five foot 10, 180 pounds.) Tiny, Boston's hockey hero during the late 1920s and 1930s, posted a 1.15 GAA with 12 shutouts in his rookie year and recorded four more averages below 2.00 in the next nine Bruin seasons. Over 12 years, Thompson had the league's best average four times and finished with a 2.08 career average, one of the best in history. His playoff mark of 1.88 is equally dazzling, though he won just one Stanley Cup. It came in 1929, when Thompson allowed just three goals in five games and collected three shutouts to lead the Bruins to its first championship.

3.20 B. Seven goals against
After another stellar December that saw Hasek allow just 18 goals on 393 shots for a league-leading save percentage of .954 and a paltry goals-against average of 1.45, the Dominator began 1999 with one of the worst performances of his career. On January 1, Anaheim routed the Sabres 7-2 when Hasek gave up all seven goals, the most ever scored in a game against the double MVP winner. The seven-goal whipping matched Hasek's previous high: a 7-6 loss to Vancouver on December 4, 1996.

3.21 D. 42 years old
Jacques Plante led the NHL in goals-against averages a record nine times, the last time in 1970-71, when he was 42. During that season Plante played 40 games (24-11-4) for Toronto and led the league with an amazing 1.88 average. (Unfortunately, Plante didn't win the Vezina Trophy that year. At that time, the trophy was awarded to goalkeepers of the team with the lowest average; the Maple Leafs had a collective 2.70 goals against.) Remarkably, Plante is the only netminder over age 40 to record an average below 2.00. In comparison, among current veterans, Dominik Hasek was a mere 29 years old when he netted his 1.95 average in 1993-94.

GAME 3

HOCKEY ROCKS

Perhaps the game's most famous song is Stompin' Tom Connors's "The Hockey Song." Played in arenas across Canada, the song is even a between-plays standard at rural rinks in unilingual French Quebec. At the closing ceremonies at Maple Leaf Gardens in February 1999, Stompin' Tom was there stompin' on his plywood and belting out the song's lyrics. In this game, match the song titles in the left column with their singer/composers in the right column.

(Solutions are on page 117)

Part 1

1. _____ "Big League"
2. _____ "Gretzky Rocks"
3. _____ "He Looked a Lot Like Tiger Williams"
4. _____ "The Hockey Song"
5. _____ "Fifty-Mission Cap"
6. _____ "Hockey"
7. _____ "Clear the Track, Here Comes Shack"

A. Stompin' Tom Connors
B. Jane Siberry
C. The Tragically Hip
D. The Pursuit of Happiness
E. The Secrets
F. Tom Cochrane
G. The Hanson Brothers

Part 2

1. _____ "Rock 'em Sock 'em Techno"
2. _____ "Pandemonium"
3. _____ "The Ballad of Wendel Clark"
4. _____ "Raised on Robbery"
5. _____ "Signin' with the NHL"
6. _____ "Overtime"
7. _____ The *Hockey Night in Canada* theme

A. Joni Mitchell
B. Don Cherry with BKS
C. DOA
D. Shuffle Demons
E. Bruno Gerussi
F. Tommy Hunter
G. *The Rheostatics*

4

THE GO-TO GUYS

In a crunch, coaches always know who to send over the boards: their go-to guys. These are the players who will win that all-important face-off, score the goal-ahead goal or make the save of the game. On the Anaheim Mighty Ducks, the go-to guys are Paul Kariya and Teemu Selanne, hockey's most dynamic duo. In 1996-97, Selanne (51 goals) and Kariya (44 goals) combined to score 95 of Anaheim's 245 goals, leading the Ducks to their first-ever playoffs. The highflying tandem scored two out of every five goals, or 39 per cent of Anahiem's total output. In this chapter, we send you over the boards to check out some of the game's great go-to guys.

(Answers are on page 51)

4.1   Which NHLer scored the most points during the 1990s?
       A. Brett Hull
       B. Jaromir Jagr
       C. Adam Oates
       D. Wayne Gretzky

4.2.   Which old-time sniper had the NHL's new goal-scoring trophy named after him in 1999?
       A. Gordie Howe
       B. Maurice Richard
       C. Bobby Hull
       D. Howie Morenz

4.3   What was Brett Hull's goal average during his 10 complete seasons with the St. Louis Blues?
       A. 44 goals per season
       B. 48 goals per season
       C. 52 goals per season
       D. 56 goals per season

4.4 Which scoring champion in the 1990s recorded the lowest full season point total since 1967-68?
A. Mario Lemieux in 1991-92
B. Wayne Gretzky in 1993-94
C. Mario Lemieux in 1996-97
D. Jaromir Jagr in 1997-98

4.5 Who was the last NHLer to win the scoring championship by recording more goals than assists?
A. Jaromir Jagr in 1994-95
B. Phil Esposito in 1970-71
C. Bobby Hull in 1965-66
D. Bernie Geoffrion in 1960-61

4.6 As of 1998-99, which two defensemen had produced the most 20-goal seasons?
A. Bobby Orr and Paul Coffey
B. Paul Coffey and Denis Potvin
C. Denis Potvin and Ray Bourque
D. Ray Bourque and Bobby Orr

4.7 How many players scored their 300th career goal faster than Teemu Selanne?
A. None
B. Only one player, Wayne Gretzky
C. Three players
D. Five players

4.8 In 1998-99, which Toronto player tied Mario Lemieux's NHL record for regular-season overtime winners?
A. Igor Korolev
B. Derek King
C. Mats Sundin
D. Steve Thomas

4.9 Which NHLer scored the highest number of goals in his career without ever posting a 50-goal season?
A. Gordie Howe
B. Bryan Hextall
C. Wayne Gretzky
D. Phil Esposito

4.10 How many goals did Jari Kurri score from Wayne Gretzky passes during his 601-goal career?
A. 100 to 200 goals
B. 200 to 300 goals
C. 300 to 400 goals
D. 400 to 500 goals

4.11 After Wayne Gretzky, which NHLer is the next-fastest 200-goal scorer?
A. Mario Lemieux
B. Mike Bossy
C. Eric Lindros
D. Brett Hull

4.12 Only two players, Wayne Gretzky and Gordie Howe, have reached the 800-goal plateau. How many NHLers, including Gretzky and Howe, have scored 700 or more goals?
A. Only Wayne Gretzky and Gordie Howe
B. Three players
C. Four players
D. Five players

4.13 After Paul Coffey, Ray Bourque and Denis Potvin, who was the fourth defenseman to score 300 career goals?
A. Phil Housley
B. Al MacInnis
C. Chris Chelios
D. Larry Murphy

4.14 Among the five players in the NHL's prestigious 700-goal club, who is the only member never elected to either the First or Second All-Star Teams?
A. Gordie Howe
B. Marcel Dionne
C. Phil Esposito
D. Mike Gartner

4.15 According to Wayne Gretzky, what percentage of his assists come from him setting up behind the net?
A. 20 per cent
B. 40 per cent
C. 60 per cent
D. 80 per cent

4.16 Who is the NHL's top point-scoring Swedish player of all time?
A. Kent Nilsson
B. Tomas Sandstrom
C. Mats Naslund
D. Mats Sundin

4.17 Who was the first NHLer to break the 50-point barrier in regular-season action?
A. Howie Morenz
B. Newsy Lalonde
C. Babe Dye
D. Nels Stewart

4.18 How many rookie points did Teemu Selanne score in 1992-93 to pass Peter Stastny's old NHL rookie record of 109 points, set in 1980-81?
A. 112 points
B. 122 points
C. 132 points
D. 142 points

4.19 Who is the youngest first-overall draft pick in NHL history?
A. Pierre Turgeon in 1987
B. Mike Modano in 1988
C. Ed Jovanovski in 1994
D. Joe Thornton in 1997

4.20 Which two players was longtime Boston general manager Harry Sinden referring to when he said, "If I'm down a goal late in the game, I want ___ on the ice. If I'm up a goal late in the game, ___'s the one I want out there."
A. Phil Esposito—Bobby Orr
B. Bobby Orr—Ray Bourque
C. Ray Bouque—Cam Neely
D. Cam Neely—Phil Esposito

4.21 Which NHLer traded midseason holds the distinction of scoring the most points during the season of his trade?
A. Jean Ratelle with Boston and the New York Rangers in 1975-76
B. Bernie Nicholls with Los Angeles and the New York Rangers in 1989-90
C. John LeClair with Montreal and Philadelphia in 1994-95
D. Teemu Selanne with Winnipeg and Anaheim in 1995-96

4.22 How many games did Theo Fleury play as a Calgary Flame (before his trade to Colorado in March 1999) after he became the Flames' all-time leading point producer?
A. One game
B. Four games
C. Eight games
D. 16 games

4.23 In what year did Europeans first sweep first, second and third place in NHL scoring?
A. 1993-94
B. 1995-96
C. 1997-98
D. 1998-99

4.24 Which sniper has finished runner-up in NHL scoring the most times?
A. Maurice Richard
B. Ted Lindsay
C. Bobby Hull
D. Marcel Dionne

THE GO-TO GUYS
Answers

4.1 **D. Wayne Gretzky**
Well past his glory days in Edmonton, the Great One still racked up the most points between 1989-90 and 1998-99. In 713 games, Gretzky scored 1,020 points for a point-per-game average of 1.43. Second only to No. 99 during the 1990s is playmaker Adam Oates, who, like Gretzky, scored almost three times as many assists as points while centring three of the league's top gunners: Brett Hull in St. Louis, Cam Neely in Boston and Peter Bondra in Washington.

The NHL's Top Scorers of the 1990s						
Player	**Teams**	**GP**	**G**	**A**	**PTS**	**PPG**
Wayne Gretzky	LA, St.L, NYR	713	257	763	1,020	1.43
Adam Oates	St.L, Bos, Wsh	721	234	693	927	1.29
Steve Yzerman	Detroit	743	363	555	918	1.27
Joe Sakic	Que, Col	722	352	565	917	1.27
Brett Hull	St.L., Dallas	713	512	384	896	1.26
Jaromir Jagr*	Pittsburgh	662	345	517	862	1.30
Mark Recchi	Pit, Phi, Mtl	766	332	508	840	1.10

Jagr played one season less (his career began in 1990-91). He is sixth in point totals but second to Gretzky in PPG during the decade.

4.2 **B. Maurice Richard**
The NHL rewards everyone, from the league-leading point earners to the plus-minus men, but until the league unveiled the Maurice Richard Trophy at the 1999 All-Star game there had never been an annual trophy for the top goal scorer. The idea

for a trophy dedicated to Richard took off in 1998, after reports that hockey's purest marksman was suffering from a rare form of stomach cancer. Canadian sportscaster Gord Miller of TSN proposed a goal scorer's trophy; Montreal Canadiens president Ronald Corey took a 200,000-signature petition to NHL commissioner Gary Bettman. The trophy weighs 30 pounds and has 50 name-plates, representing Richard's league-first 50 goals in 50 games in 1944-45. There are nine levels, for his famous No. 9 jersey. The centrepiece is a bronze statue of Richard. The inscription reads, "Never give up"—Richard's motto as a player and, later, as a cancer survivor. The first winner of the Marice Richard Trophy was Anaheim's Teemu Selanne.

4.3   C. 52 goals per season

After being acquired at the 1988 trade deadline by St. Louis, Hull went on to lead the league in goal scoring three straight years, and eventually scored 521 times in 731 games with the Blues between 1988-89 and 1997-98. Hull averaged 52 .1 goals per season during his 10-year career in St. Louis.

4.4   D. Jaromir Jagr in 1997-98

Although Jaromir Jagr led the NHL with 102 points in 1997-98, it was the lowest total by a scoring leader (with the exception of the NHL lockout-shortened year, 1994-95) since 1967-68, when Stan Mikita recorded a league-high 87 points. Jagr's totals are indicative of league-wide scoring trends, which dipped to 5.28 goals per game in 1997-98, the lowest average in 42 years.

4.5   C. Bobby Hull in 1965-66

No player has won the scoring title by recording more goals than assists since Bobby Hull's 54-43-97 season in 1965-66. Geoffrion did it in 1960-61 (50-45-95), when he became the second NHLer to score 50 goals in one season; Esposito had the same number of goals and assists in his record-breaking 76-76-152 season of 1970-71; Jagr came the closest in recent times during the player lockout of 1994-95, with 32 goals and 38 assists in 48 games.

4.6   C. Denis Potvin and Ray Bourque

Bobby Orr could have won this race had his surgery-ravaged knees not given out after nine seasons. Orr recorded seven consecutive 20-or-more-goal years during his brief career, two less than the league-leading nine seasons set by Ray Bourque (through 19 plus seasons) and Denis Potvin. Bourque might have been the runaway leader in this category had he scored just one goal more in each of four 19-goal seasons during his career. Coffey produced eight 20-goal years and Al MacInnis, six.

4.7   D. Five players

Only Wayne Gretzky, Mario Lemieux, Brett Hull, Mike Bossy and Jari Kurri scored career goal number 300 faster than Selanne. Selanne became the sixth-fastest player in league history to reach the 300 mark on February 27, 1999, when he pegged his 300th NHL goal against San Jose in a 4-1 Anaheim win. It was Selanne's 464th NHL game.

4.8   D. Steve Thomas

Steve Thomas's ninth career overtime goal on February 20, 1999, not only tied him with Mario Lemieux for the all-time high in overtime winners, the goal represented another milestone: the first game-winning goal and first extra-period winner at the new $265-million Air Canada Centre in Toronto. The Maple Leafs won their first home game at the Hangar, defeating their longtime rivals, the Montreal Canadiens, 3-2 on Thomas's goal at 3:48 in overtime.

4.9   A. Gordie Howe

In the 1950s the most commonly debated hockey question was: Who is the better player, Gordie Howe or Maurice Richard? For all their scoring success, both Richard and Howe suffered a major disappointment in their careers. Richard, hockey's first 50-goal scorer, never won an NHL scoring championship; Howe, a four-time league scoring leader, failed to notch a 50-goal season despite scoring 801 goals. But both came agonizingly close to realizing their dreams: Richard missed the scoring title by one point in 1954-55; Howe totalled 49 goals in 1952-53.

4.10 C. 300 to 400 goals

In 13 NHL seasons together, hockey's greatest playmaker and one of its best scorers teamed up to put a lot of pucks in the net. The Gretzky-Kurri unit began in earnest January 11, 1981, against the Nordiques in Quebec City. Kurri scored three times, all on assists from Gretzky. After that, the Great One helped Kurri score 364 goals in 13 seasons with Edmonton and Los Angeles. Meanwhile, Gretzky reached his famed 802nd career goal, aided by 194 assists from Kurri.

4.11 B. Mike Bossy

While Gretzky needed just 242 games to score goal number 200, the Islanders' Mike Bossy took only 13 games more, whacking home number 200 in his 255th game in 1980-81. Lemieux needed 277 games, Hull 280 and Lindros 307 (the fifth-fewest game total by any 200-goal man in league history).

4.12 D. Five players

As of 1998-99, only five NHLers have scored more than 700 regular-season goals in league history. The most recent was Mike Gartner, who notched number 700 on December 14, 1997, in his 1,390th game. The historic goal came against Chris Osgood during the 3-3 match with Detroit. Later, Gartner scored his 701st with fewer than five minutes remaining in regulation time, to give the Coyotes the tie.

The NHL's 700-Goal Club*

Player	Team	Year	NHL Season	Age	TG
Gordie Howe	Det	1968-69	23rd	40	801
Phil Esposito	NYR	1979-80	17th	38	701
Marcel Dionne	LA	1987-88	17th	36	731
Wayne Gretzky	LA	1990-91	12th	30	894
Mike Gartner	Pho	1997-98	19th	38	708

Current to 1998-99

4.13 A. Phil Housley

Housley, of the Calgary Flames, became only the fourth defenseman in league history to reach the 300-goal plateau in a 3-1 loss to Chicago, March 17, 1999. "It's a great feeling to be in that crowd, with those great players," said Housley, who had six goals in his last 15 games (after scoring only three in his first 52 of 1998-99) to reach the career milestone. D-man Al MacInnis is next up to hit the all-time-high benchmark for career goals; he should notch his 300th in 1999-2000.

4.14 D. Mike Gartner

In his 19-year NHL career, Gartner was never selected to a First or Second All-Star Team. He is the only member in the elite 700-goal club without All-Star status. Gretzky had a combined 14 All-Star selections; Howe, 21; Esposito, eight; and Dionne, four.

4.15 B. 40 per cent

Gretzky's so-called "office" on-ice was behind the net, where he scored most of his assists. The strategy started in Junior B hockey after Gretzky kept getting knocked over by bigger defensemen. At the suggestion of his coach, Gretzky began setting up behind the net, much like Bobby Clarke was doing with the Philadelphia Flyers. The net offered Gretzky protection but also made defenders turn their backs on his teammates, causing breakdowns that led to Gretzky-assisted goals. "Forty per cent (of my assists) have come from behind the net. The next biggest number would be hitting the late guy. Between those two plays, I'd say that probably accounted for three-quarters of my assists," says Gretzky.

4.16 B. Tomas Sandstrom

As of 1998-99, Sandstrom is the highest-scoring Swede in NHL history. Drafted in the second round by New York in 1982, Sandstrom led the Rangers with 29 goals and finished third in rookie goal scoring behind Mario Lemieux (43 goals) and War-ren Young (40) in 1984-85. Sandstrom scored a career-high 45 goals in 1990-91, and is tied for second place in the NHL record books with eight overtime goals. Born in Finland and raised a

Swede, Sandstrom won a bronze medal with Sweden at the 1984 Winter Olympics in Sarajevo. In 1997, he helped Detroit win its first Stanley Cup since 1955.

The NHL's Highest-Scoring Swedes*				
Player	Years	G	A	Pts
Tomas Sandstrom	1984-1999	394	462	856
Mats Sundin	1990-1999	296	419	715
Kent Nilsson	1979-1995	264	422	686
Mats Naslund	1982-1995	251	383	634
Hakan Loob	1983-1989	193	236	429
* Current to 1998-99				

4.17 A. Howie Morenz

Morenz became the first 50-point man in the NHL's 11th season, 1927-28, scoring 33 goals and 18 assists for 51 points in the 44-game schedule. Known as the Babe Ruth of hockey, Morenz caught the eye of New York promoters who, after witnessing his blinding speed and the stunning effect his play had on hockey crowds, concluded that Madison Square Garden should be turned into a hockey arena and that New York needed to organize its own club, the Rangers.

4.18 C. 132 points

In NHL history no rookie has ever matched Selanne for sheer impact on the record books. In his freshman campaign he was christened the Finnish Flash, after scoring an unprecedented 132 points, 23 more than Stastny's old record of 109 points. Selanne's 76 goals led the league and he topped Mike Bossy's rookie mark (53 goals) by 23 goals. Moreover, Selanne's goal count was the fifth-highest total in history. His scoring streaks that year awed the hockey world; in one 17-game stretch he netted 20 goals and 14 assists. So how did an NHL rookie from the Finnish Elite League produce such a dramatic start? At 22, he was almost three years older than the average rookie and, therefore, far more mature and prepared. His scoring consistency under the grind of an 84-game schedule attested to this readiness and maturity, to say nothing of his hockey skills.

4.19 A. Pierre Turgeon in 1987

Turgeon, of the Granby Bisons, was 17 years and 10 months old when he was selected first overall by the Buffalo Sabres on his draft day in 1997. Brian Bellows was also just 17 years and 10 months old when he was picked at the 1982 Entry Draft. But Bellows was chosen second overall by Minnesota. Joe Thornton was just a month older than Turgeon on his draft day in 1997.

The NHL's Youngest No. 1 Draft Picks*				
Player	**Year**	**Drafted by**	**Drafted from**	**Age**
Pierre Turgeon	1987	Buffalo	Granby Bisons	17.10
Joe Thornton	1997	Boston	Sault Ste. Marie Greyhounds	17.11
Mike Modano	1988	Minnesota	Prince Albert Raiders	18.0
Ed Jovanovski	1994	Florida	Windsor Spitfires	18.0
Dale Hawerchuk	1981	Winnipeg	Cornwall Royals	18.2
Roman Hamrlik	1992	Tampa Bay	ZPS Zlin (Czech.)	18.2
Vincent Lecavalier	1998	Tampa Bay	Rimouski Oceanic	18.2

Current to 1998-99

4.20 B. Bobby Orr—Ray Bourque

Harry Sinden, the Bruins' general manager since 1972-73 and Stanley Cup-winning coach, once said, "If I'm down a goal late in the game, I want Orr on the ice. If I'm up a goal late in the game, Bourque's the one I want out there." Sinden should know, having been around long enough to have the privilege of utilizing two of hockey's greatest offensive defensemen. Orr could always be counted on to score the big ones when Boston needed it most and Bourque was the Bruins' most dependable defender.

4.21 B. Bernie Nicholls with Los Angeles and the New York Rangers in 1989-90

One season after he posted his career year (150 points in 1988-89 with Wayne Gretzky in Los Angeles), the Kings traded

Nicholls midseason to New York for Tony Granato and Tomas Sandstrom on January 20, 1990. It proved to be Nicholls's second-best season ever: he scored 112 points between the Kings and the Rangers, the highest point total for a player traded midseason.

The Highest Point Totals for Players Traded Midseason*

Player	Season	Teams	GP	G	A	PTS	TP
Bernie Nicholls	1989-90	LA	47	27	48	75	
		NYR	32	12	25	37	112
John Cullen	1990-91	Pit	65	31	63	94	
		Htf	13	8	8	16	110
Teemu Selanne	1995-96	Wpg	51	24	48	72	
		Ana	28	16	20	36	108
Jean Ratelle	1974-75	NYR	13	5	10	15	
		Bos	67	31	59	98	105
Adam Oates	1991-92	St. L	54	10	59	69	
		Bos	26	10	20	30	99
Dave Andreychuk	1992-93	Buf	52	29	32	61	
		Tor	31	25	13	38	99

* Current to 1998-99

4.22 B. Four games

After almost 800 games and more than 11 seasons as a Flame, Fleury became Calgary's all-time leading scorer on February 19, 1999, just nine days and four matches before he was traded to Colorado, February 28. The milestone goal, a shorthanded marker between the legs of Anaheim goalie Guy Hebert, was Fleury's 823rd point, one more than Al MacInnis's club record of 822. Fleury's final tally in Calgary was 830 points.

4.23 C. 1997-98

In 1997-98, with Wayne Gretzky in his 19th season, Mario Lemieux retired, Paul Kariya injured and only a few other

North American scoring stars (Canadian Eric Lindros and American John LeClair) in the race, the NHL witnessed its first trio of Europeans to sweep the top scoring positions. Czech-born Jaromir Jagr (102 points), Peter Forsberg of Sweden (91 points) and Russian Pavel Bure (90 points) finished one-two-three, followed by Gretzky (in a tie with Bure) and LeClair (87 points). In 1994-95, Jagr became the first European to win the NHL scoring title. The runner-up that year was Lindros.

4.24 A. Maurice Richard

Interestingly, the player whose name is honoured on the new NHL goal-scoring award never won the Art Ross Trophy as the league's point-scoring champion. Not that Richard wasn't trying or anything. But, as the game's leading goal scorer, Richard was often outpointed by players who amassed greater point totals based on bigger numbers in the assist column than the goal column. For Richard, who usually recorded more goals than assists in a season, missing the Art Ross was his greatest disappointment. He finished second a record five times; twice, just one point behind the top scorer (including 1954-55, when Richard lost to teammate Bernie Geoffrion after being suspended for striking an official). Only old-timer Cy Denneny ties Richard for most runner-up finishes. But while Denneny also finished second five times, he did win a scoring championship (1923-24).

GAME 4
THE LUCKY 13

The 500th career goal has become an NHL standard of greatness. Among the 27 players who recorded 500 or more goals before the year 2000, 13 hit the millennium mark during the 1990s. In this game find the lucky 13 in the puzzle by reading across, down or diagonally. As with our example of Steve Y-Z-E-R-M-A-N, connect each last name using letters no more than once. Start with the letters printed in heavy type.

(Solutions are on page 117)

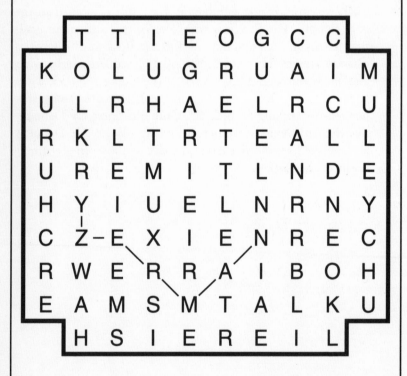

5

TRUE OR FALSE?

No NHLer has ever scored a hat trick in overtime. True or False? Unlike today, in hockey's early days a tied game after three periods meant a mandatory 10 minutes of overtime—whether or not one or more goals were scored. On January 16, 1934, Ken Doraty potted a hat trick in the 10-minute overtime to lead the Maple Leafs to a 7-4 victory over the Ottawa Senators. In this chapter, we change pace with a true or false lineup of questions that will keep *you* working overtime. (By the way, Doraty had a penchant for extra periods. He also scored the playoff game winner against Boston the previous year, 1933, after a record 104 minutes and 46 seconds of overtime.)

(Answers are on page 64)

5.1 Wayne Gretzky scored his first 50th goal the same night Guy Lafleur scored his last 50th. *True or False?*

5.2 In 1998-99, the Detroit Red Wings paid Sergei Fedorov more than Nashville paid its entire roster of Predators. *True or False?*

5.3 No goalie has ever worn sweater No. 0. *True or False?*

5.4 The province of Quebec has produced the most players in the Hockey Hall of Fame. *True or False?*

5.5 The goal that defeated the Toronto Maple Leafs in their last game at Maple Leaf Gardens was scored by former Leaf captain Doug Gilmour. *True or False?*

5.6 No NHLer has ever taken penalty shots for two different teams in one season. *True or False?*

5.7 No coach has ever coached in all three major junior leagues in Canada. *True or False?*

5.8 The St. Louis Blues had the NHL's worst power play in 1998-99, the season after they lost Brett Hull and Steve Duchesne. *True or False?*

5.9 There are fewer fights per game when two referees (as opposed to one referee) officiate NHL matches. *True or False?*

5.10 The amount of fighting in the NHL increased during the 1990s. *True or False?*

5.11 Hockey is the only major team sport that permits fighting. *True or False?*

5.12 It is illegal to play street hockey in some Montreal suburbs. *True or False?*

5.13 No player in NHL history has ever recorded a power-play goal in overtime in playoff action. *True or False?*

5.14 During his career, Bobby Orr accumulated more penalty minutes than total points. *True or False?*

5.15 Terry Sawchuk was with the Detroit Red Wings when he became the first NHL goalie to record 400 wins. *True or False?*

5.16 Wayne Gretzky scored the most points by a visiting player in the history of Toronto's Maple Leaf Gardens. *True or False?*

5.17 Tough guy Stu Grimson never recorded a two-goal night. *True or False?*

5.18 In 1999, a company unveiled a new hockey stick with a crooked shaft. *True or False?*

5.19 The first NHL team in Pittsburgh was the Penguins. *True or False?*

5.20 No one who saw the New York Rangers win the Stanley Cup at Madison Square Garden in 1994, also witnessed the Rangers' previous Cup victory 54 years earlier in 1940. *True or False?*

5.21 Theoren Fleury was the last player remaining from the Calgary Flames' Stanley Cup-winning team of 1988-89. *True or False?*

5.22 Trevor Kidd was chosen ahead of Martin Brodeur in the 1990 NHL Entry Draft. *True or False?*

5.23 All of Tony Esposito's 76 shutouts came with Chicago, where he played all but 13 games of his 886-game career. *True or False?*

5.24 Despite being donated by Maple Leaf Gardens in 1965 to honour the Maple Leafs' founder, the Conn Smythe Trophy (playoff MVP) has never been won by a Toronto Maple Leaf player. *True or False?*

5.25 Among all Stanley Cup-winning teams, the 1989 Calgary Flames had the most players whose surnames began with "Mac" or "Mc." *True or False?*

5.26 Every time the New York Rangers captured the Stanley Cup, they won the Cup-clinching game by a one-goal margin. *True or False?*

5.27 Wayne Gretzky is the only player in NHL history to win the Hart Trophy as league MVP with two different teams. *True or False?*

5.28 The first NHLer awarded a penalty shot in the Stanley Cup finals was an American. *True or False?*

5.29 Tony Esposito is the oldest goalie to hit 400 wins. *True or False?*

5.30 No team has ever sported one regular line with three 50-goal scorers. *True or False?*

5.31 The oldest NHL arena—once Toronto moved out of Maple Leaf Gardens in 1999—was the Civic Arena in Pittsburgh. *True or False?*

TRUE OR FALSE?
Answers

5.1 **True**

The torch was truly passed from one era's superstar to the next on April 2, 1980, when Lafleur and Gretzky each scored their 50th goals of the season. It was the sixth and final time Lafleur would score 50 and the first of nine for the Great One.

5.2 **True**

Fedorov earned $14 million from Detroit—almost half a million more than the $13.6 million the Predators paid to ice its entire team in its first year of expansion, 1998-99.

5.3 **False**

Paul Bibeault, a journeyman goaltender through the war years, wore jersey No. 0 with the Montreal Canadiens in 1942-43. Bibeault played the entire 50-game schedule, but on some nights he donned No. 1, too. New York Ranger netminder John Davidson wore double zeroes on his jersey for one season in the 1970s.

5.4 **False**

Of the 214 greats inducted into the Hockey Hall of Fame between 1945 and 1998, 108 players were born in Ontario. Quebec ranks second with 49 players; Manitoba has 18; Saskatchewan, 15; Alberta, seven: British Columbia, two; and Newfoundland and New Brunswick, one each. Only four American states can boast Hall of Famers. Minnesota has two native sons in the Hall; Kansas, New York and Pennsylvania, one apiece.

5.5 True

Wearing the "A" for Chicago, Gilmour, once the heart and soul of the Maple Leafs, scored the Blackhawks' game winner against Toronto at the Maple Leaf Gardens' finale, February 13, 1999. Gilmour scored the Hawks' third goal in the 6-2 victory.

5.6 False

In 1994-95, Mark Recchi became the first player awarded penalty shots for two different teams in a single season. Recchi, playing with Philadelphia, was stopped by Ottawa's Don Beaupre on February 6, 1995. A month later on March 8, as a Montreal Canadien, Recchi missed scoring in a one-on-one against Dominik Hasek.

5.7 False

As of 1998-99, the only person to have coached in all three Canadian major junior leagues, the OHL, QMJHL and WHL, is "Travellin'" Joe Canale. At age 49, Canale had been a bench boss with seven major junior teams across Canada, including the Medicine Hat Tigers of the WHL, the Sarnia Sting of the OHL and five teams (Sherbrooke, Laval, Chicoutimi, Beauport and Shawnigan) in the QMJHL. Canale coached Canada's national junior team to two golds at the World Junior Championships in 1993 (as assistant coach) and 1994 (as head coach). Many future NHLers played under his tutelage, including Paul Kariya, Chris Pronger and Eric Daze.

5.8 False

Despite losing power-play snipers Hull and Duchesne, the Blues had the league's third-most productive specialty unit in manpower advantage situations in 1998-99. "It can be a strange thing," said captain Chris Pronger. "Sometimes, when you have too much skill or too many skilled players, you try to make it too pretty and it doesn't work." The Blues were number three in the league (just behind Anaheim, 22.0, and the Rangers, 20.4) with a 20.3 per cent success rate. The previous season St. Louis finished ninth with a 16.8 per cent ratio.

5.9 True

The two-referee system affects not only fighting but penalty box times and length of games. In 1998-99, the NHL employed two referees in 25 per cent of its games. Fighting took a nose-dive, dropping from .650 fights per game with one referee to .550 with two referees. Games with two officials averaged 32.5 minutes in penalties called; those with one had 33.1 minutes. The game length also varied: two referees sped up the game by two minutes, from 156 minutes (two hours 36 minutes) to 154 minutes.

5.10 False

In the 10-year period between 1989-90 and 1998-99, fighting decreased dramatically: from .914 to .620 fights per game. Fisticuffs took a nosedive in 1992-93 to .624, when the new instigator rule was implemented. The measure ejects player(s) who instigate a fight.

5.11 True

No other major team sport allows fisticuffs. In fact, the NHL is the only major sports league to acknowledge fighting as part of the game, and that doesn't punish fighters with immediate expulsion. The basic penalty is five minutes for fighting. Perhaps the only time there is an absence of fighting in the NHL is when winning matters most: at the Stanley Cup playoffs.

5.12 True

In September 1998 three teens in Longueuil, a community southeast of Montreal, were fined for playing street hockey. After being warned by a parking inspector that road hockey was breaking a municipal by-law, the police were called and the three boys were fined $130 each. Go figure.

5.13 False

A power-play goal in overtime in the playoffs? It's rare for an official to call a penalty in postseason in an overtime situation; even rarer for a power-play goal to occur as a result. But it has happened. On March 28, 1933, the Bruins' George Owen hauled down Bill Thoms of the Maple Leafs in a 0-0 overtime deadlock. On the subsequent play, with Owen in the box, Busher Jackson scored on a pass from Thoms to give Toronto the 1-0 win.

5.14 True

Bobby Orr, the only defenseman in NHL history to lead the league in scoring and the only player besides Wayne Gretzky and Mario Lemieux to earn more than 100 assists in a season, amassed more minutes in the box than points on the scoreboard. Orr collected 915 points and 953 penalty minutes during his 12-year career.

5.15 False

Sawchuk recorded win number 400 on February 4, 1965, in a 5-2 victory over Montreal. He was a Toronto Maple Leaf at the time.

5.16 True

In 30 regular-season appearances at the Gardens, Gretzky scored 77 points (30 goals, 47 assists), the most by any visiting player. The Great One scored his last two points on assists during his final visit to MLG on December 19, 1998, as the Rangers lost to Toronto 7-4.

5.17 False

On October 27, 1998, Grimson of the Mighty Ducks made personal history and scored two goals (including one that went in off his skate) in three minutes during a 5-2 win over Tampa Bay. Grimson, who averages one goal every 56 games (or nine goals in 510 career games), jokingly remarked, "Do I have any scoring clauses in my contract? I've got to call my agent."

5.18 True

In February 1999, International Marketing Management of Oak Park, Illinois, introduced the UB Offset. The stick has a "hands forward" design: a shaft that snakes back half an inch just above the heel of the blade. According to the company, the UB Offset improves passing, shooting and stickhandling because the design allows players to hold the puck further back in their stance. The UB Offset has been approved for use in the NHL and IHL. The first pro player to use it was Chicago Wolves defenseman Steve Gosselin.

5.19 False

Hockey has a long history in Pittsburgh. In fact, even before Detroit or Chicago owned NHL franchises, the Steel City boasted the Pirates, the NHL's third U.S. club (after the Boston Bruins and New York Americans). The Pirates began operations in 1925-26 under the ownership of ex-boxer Benny Leonard and the coaching of NHL tough guy Odie Cleghorn. The roster was stocked with amateurs, including Lionel Conacher, Baldy Cotton and Roy Worters, all from Pittsburgh's United States Amateur Hockey Association championship team, the Yellow Jackets. The Pirates played five NHL seasons before poor fan support and the 1929 stock market crash wiped out the franchise. It would be 37 years before the NHL returned to Pittsburgh, with the Penguins in 1967.

5.20 False

Longtime New York hockey writer Norm MacLean and broadcaster Dick Irvin, Jr. each witnessed both Ranger Cups, the first at Maple Leaf Gardens in 1940 and the next, 54 years later, at Madison Square Garden. MacLean, at age 10, travelled to Toronto with his father to see the deciding game in 1940; Irvin, Jr., at age eight, was on hand as the son of Dick Irvin, coach of the losing Maple Leafs.

5.21 True

Theo Fleury became the last active member from the 1989 Stanley Cup-winning Calgary Flames when the second-to-last remaining Cup winner, Gary Roberts, was traded to the Carolina Hurricanes on August 25, 1997. Calgary put its championship legacy to rest when Fleury was dealt to Colorado February 28, 1999.

5.22 True

Calgary might have made the most important draft swap of its franchise when it flipped first-round draft positions with New Jersey in 1990. The Flames moved to 11th overall and the Devils to 22nd. Both teams sought goaltenders but Calgary failed to capitalize on its improved position, grabbing Trevor Kidd instead of the player who would become New Jersey's later choice, Martin Brodeur. Brodeur led New Jersey to the Stanley Cup in 1995, while Kidd played four mediocre seasons with the Flames before being traded to Carolina in 1997.

5.23 False

Esposito is seventh among all-time shutout leaders with 76, but two of those shutouts came in Montreal where he played the first 13 games of his 16-year NHL career.

5.24 False

Since the Conn Smythe was first awarded in 1965, only one Maple Leaf has won the trophy honouring that club's founder, the coach and builder of Maple Leaf Gardens. Toronto's Dave Keon was named playoff MVP of 1967 after a sensational post-season against Chicago and Montreal. Keon, an aggressive two-way centre, frustrated highly favoured Montreal in the Stanley Cup finals with his checking and defensive work. He also scored a goal and an assist as Toronto surprised the Canadiens to capture the Cup.

5.25 True

The 1988-89 Flames could have started a pipe band with all the "Macs" and "Mcs" on their squad. More than 20 per cent of the 24-member team had last names beginning in Mac or Mc, the prefix of Scottish and Irish surnames. The five Flames were Al MacInnis, Brad McCrimmon, Lanny McDonald, Brian MacLellan and Jamie Macoun. The number rises to six if you count Calgary's assistant general manager, Al MacNeil.

5.26 True

As of 1998-99, the Rangers have won four Stanley Cups, all by one-goal margins! Two goals of the series were pushed to the deciding match and the other two came in overtime victories. Similar to 1994's heartstopping 3-2 victory over Vancouver in Game 7, in 1928 New York captured their first Cup in the fifth and final game of the best-of-five series with a close 2-1 win over the Montreal Maroons. In 1933 and 1940, the Rangers won the Cup again, edging their opponents by one-goal margins. On both occasions the Maple Leafs fell victim in tight 1-0 and 3-2 overtime losses.

5.27 False

Although Gretzky won MVP status on multiple occasions with Edmonton (eight times) and once in Los Angeles, he is not the only NHLer so distinguished. Mark Messier's two Harts were split between Edmonton (1990) and New York (1992).

5.28 True

The first penalty shot awarded in Cup finals action came on April 13, 1944, when Montreal's Bill Durnan stopped Chicago's Virgil Johnson. Johnson, one of only four Americans (along with Frank Brimsek, Billy Moe and John Mariucci) playing in the NHL, was from Minneapolis.

5.29 False

Only six netminders have broken the 400-win mark. The oldest was Jacques Plante, who recorded win number 400 at the age of 42; Esposito and Hall, the next oldest, were both 40 years old.

5.30 True

Although the Edmonton Oilers are the first team to feature three 50-goal scorers in one season (Wayne Gretzky, Jari Kurri and Glenn Anderson in 1983-84), no club has ever produced one scoring line with such offensive power. The Buffalo Sabres may have come the closest in 1992-93, when they combined Pat LaFontaine, Alexander Mogilny and Dave Andreychuk as a unit. Poised to become the NHL's first three 50-goal scorers on a line, the Sabres traded Andreychuk to Toronto. Mogilny finished the year with 76 goals, LaFontaine, 53 and Andreychuk, in Toronto, scored 54.

5.31 True
When Maple Leaf Gardens, the last of the great barns of the Original Six era, closed its doors in February 1999, the NHL's oldest arena became the 37-year-old Civic Arena in Pittsburgh, home of the Penguins since 1967.

GAME 5

TWIN PEAKS

How many NHL snipers have reached the twin peaks of winning the Art Ross Trophy as scoring leader and the Hart Trophy as league MVP in one season? In this game, 16 of the 17 double-award winners listed below appear in the puzzle horizontally, vertically or backwards. Some are easily found, such as MARIO; others require a more careful search. After you have circled all 32 *first* and *last* names and the trophy names, Art Ross and Hart, read the remaining eight letters in descending order to spell the only defenseman in NHL history to claim Art Ross/Hart status at season's end. To get started, here is a list of the first names that need to be circled; fill in the last names and circle them in the puzzle, too.

(Solutions are on page 118)

Mario _____

Wayne _____

Nels_____

Jean _____

Bobby _____

Phil _____

Brian _____

Elmer _____

Bernie _____

Howie _____

Stan _____

Bill _____

Max _____

Guy _____

Toe _____

Gordie _____

```
Y E L W O C G R E T Z K Y
B L A K E E N Y A W Z B Y
B M C X U E I M E L N E E
O E H A R T M N S O E L L
B R Y A N A A T I M R I T
B A B E R E E R A O O V N
I R E I J W F X B B M E E
L T O N A F M N E L S A B
L R T R O T T I E R L U L
H O T E N A T S K Y O U I
O S G B R Y U G E I W O H
W S E S P O S I T O T R P
E I D R O G R U E L F A L
```

6

READER REBOUND

In the previous hockey trivia book in this series we asked readers to contribute their own questions, by filling out the form at the back of the book. We received mail from hockey fans all over North America (and one letter from Australia), some of which we've answered in this year's book. Congratulations and thanks to all those who participated. If you didn't make the final cut in this edition, please try again next season. *(Answers are on page 76)*

6.1 Who is the only NHL goalie credited with a goal and a shutout in the same game?

Tim Spear
Nepean, Ontario

6.2 Who was the first NHLer to score an NHL goal in a game outside of North America?

Jody Crane
Sardis, British Columbia

6.3 Who scored the last NHL goal of the Original Six era before league expansion in 1967?

Donald Theriault
Dartmouth, Nova Scotia

6.4 Who was the only non-captain to score a goal in Game 7 of the 1994 Cup finals?

Kyle Vince Mullins
Valley Stream, New York

6.5 Name the only NHL team to play in three Game 7s (out of the four best-of-seven playoff rounds) in one postseason.

Brian Cormier
St. Antoine de Kent, New Brunswick

6.6　What was Rendez-Vous '87?

Justin Messor
Salem, New Hampshire

6.7　Which rookie from among Jaromir Jagr, Mats Sundin and
　　Sergei Fedorov led the league in points in 1990-91?

Durral Wiegel
Sexsmith, Alberta

6.8　How many Stanley Cups have the Detroit Red Wings won?

Kyle Horton
Dunnville, Ontario

6.9　Who was the last NHLer to play without a helmet?

Pierre-Oliver Zappa
Montreal, Quebec

6.10　Who scored the most game-winning goals in the 1980s?

Chris Brown
Moose Jaw, Saskatchewan

6.11　Why wasn't the Stanley Cup awarded in 1919?

Beth Stevenson
Longmont, Colorado

6.12　How many goalies have captained NHL teams?

Stefan Gislason
Winnipeg, Manitoba

6.13　What is the best career goals-per-game average by a player
　　since 1893, the first year of Stanley Cup competition?

Paul Gilly
Staten Island, New York

6.14　Who was the last player to score a goal at the old Boston
　　Garden?

Douglas Anderson
Kensington, Connecticut

6.15 Who scored the first goal at the inaugural game of Boston's Fleet Center?

Emily Stone
Wellesley, Massachusetts

6.16 What is the most number of power-play goals scored by Brett Hull in one season?

Brad Sanders
Troy, Ohio

6.17 How long did it take Mario Lemieux to score his first NHL goal?

Steven Khan
Mississauga, Ontario

6.18 Which NHL sniper holds the record for the most shots on goal during a single season?

Kristen Marcott
Port Hood, Nova Scotia

6.19 In what American city did the Calgary Flames originate?

Daniel Falloon
Winnipeg, Manitoba

6.20 What is the most number of shots taken by a defenseman in a single season?

Justin McGillivary
Fergus, Ontario

READER REBOUND
Answers

6.1 **Goalie Damian Rhodes.** Rhodes almost singlehandedly carried Ottawa to victory on January 2, 1999, when he received credit for scoring a goal and recording his first shutout of the season as the Senators beat New Jersey 6-0. Rhodes was the last Ottawa player to touch the puck after the Devils' Lyle Odelein cleared it to the point and it sailed by three fellow defenders into New Jersey's vacated net. (Martin Brodeur had left the ice on a delayed penalty call.) Rhodes's feat had another twist: he is the first netminder to score on another netminder who himself had once scored a goal. Brodeur notched his goal, a playoff marker, on April 17, 1997. "The goal was like the cherry on top," said Rhodes. "But the shutout is definitely better. It's better to stop pucks than to score."

6.2 **Scott Walker.** The first time an NHL puck was dropped for a regular-season game outside North America was on October 3, 1997, when the Vancouver Canucks and Anaheim Mighty Ducks played in Tokyo, Japan. Vancouver's Scott Walker scored the game's first goal in the 3-2 Canuck win over the Ducks. A capacity crowd of 10,500 witnessed the match at Yoyogi Arena.

6.3 **George Armstrong.** The six-team era's last goal was an empty netter, scored by Toronto Maple Leaf captain George Armstrong in Game 6 of the Montreal-Toronto Stanley Cup finals on May 2, 1967. Armstrong's playoff goal clinched Toronto's 13th Stanley Cup in the 3-1 victory over the Canadiens.

6.4 **Adam Graves.** In New York's 3-2 Cup win over Vancouver in 1994, the only non-captain to score a goal in the final game was Adam Graves. The other four goals in the Cup-deciding contest were scored by Rangers captain Mark Messier, associate captain Brian Leetch and Vancouver captain Trevor Linden, who tallied the two Canuck goals.

6.5 **Toronto Maple Leafs.** No team in NHL history has played more Game 7s in a single postseason than the 1993 Toronto Maple Leafs. And they did it in three consecutive best-of-seven series without even making it to the Stanley Cup finals! The 1993 Maple Leafs squeaked by two teams—Detroit in the Divisional semis and St. Louis in the Divisional finals—thanks to seventh-game victories, before falling in their third Game 7 against the Los Angeles Kings in the Conference finals.

6.6 **A hockey superpower showdown.** Rendez-Vous '87 replaced the 1987 NHL All-Star game. Marcel Aubut, president of the Quebec Nordiques, created a huge cultural celebration centred around a two-game series pitting the NHL's best against the Soviet National Team. The NHL stars won Game 1 4-3, while the Soviets—stocked with talent bound for the NHL—took Game 2 5-3.

6.7 **Sergei Fedorov.** Despite a deep rookie crop that included the likes of Jaromir Jagr and Mats Sundin, it was Sergei Fedorov who led all freshmen in scoring, including goals (31), assists (48), points (79) and game-winning goals (5). Boston's Ken Hodge tied Sundin for second place with 59 points, an amazing 20 points back of Fedorov. Jagr was next with 57 points. Surprisingly, Fedorov didn't win the Calder Trophy as top rookie. He was runner-up to Chicago's Ed Belfour.

6.8 **Nine Stanley Cups.** Detroit's love affair with hockey dates back to the 1920s and the old Olympia Stadium. It was at the Olympia that the Red Wings became a powerhouse, winning back-to-back Stanley Cups in 1936 and 1937 and another in 1943. But the best was yet to come for Detroit fans. Red Wings manager Jack Adams assembled one of hockey's greatest dynasties in the late 1940s and 1950s, led by Gordie Howe, Ted Lindsay and Terry Sawchuk. The Wings dominated the league and won four championships in six years. In 1997 and 1998, Detroit took twin Cups at their new rink, the Joe Louis Arena, bringing their total to nine Stanley Cup championships, as of 1999. Only the Montreal Canadiens and the Toronto Maple Leafs have won Lord Stanley's trophy more often.

6.9 **Craig MacTavish.** MacTavish was the last remaining player to appear in an NHL game without a helmet. MacTavish, who had signed a player's contract prior to the 1979 cutoff date for exemption from the NHL's helmet rule, retired April 29, 1997, after 17 NHL seasons. He played in 1,093 regular-season games and 193 playoff matches.

6.10 Mike Bossy. Wayne Gretzky's scoring heroics in the 1980s left few NHL records unturned. But one mark that eluded him during the decade was most game-winning goals. Bossy, forever in the Great One's shadow, outscored No. 99 in this category, notching a record 68 game winners to Gretzky's 66. Bossy's feat is exceptional considering he played 599 games during the 1980s—175 fewer games than Gretzky's total of 774.

6.11 Flu epidemic. The only time the NHL failed to award a Stanley Cup was in 1919. The Montreal Canadiens and the Pacific Coast Hockey League champion Seattle Metropolitans played five games (two wins and a tie each) before the series was halted due to an influenza epidemic. Several players fell ill; Montreal's Joe Hall died.

6.12 Six goalie captains. There hasn't been a goalie captain in more than 50 years. Their tenure ended in 1948 when Bill Durnan captained Montreal in the 1947-48 season. Durnan created so many unscheduled timeouts for the Canadiens (by leaving his crease to question the referee on calls) that other teams complained. The next season the NHL passed a rule prohibiting netminders from serving as captains or associate captains. Prior to Durnan, five other goalies proudly wore the "C": John Ross Roach of the Toronto St. Pats, Roy Worters of the New York Americans, George Hainsworth of the Montreal Canadiens, Alex Connell of the Ottawa Senators and Chuck Gardiner of the Chicago Blackhawks.

6.13 Three goals per game. The name Russell Bowie doesn't spring to mind when we think of great goal scorers. He never won an NHL scoring title, an individual award or received MVP status. But his name is enshrined in the Hockey Hall of Fame; if you check back far enough you'll find R. Bowie amongst his peers as a Stanley Cup champion with the Montreal Victorias of 1898-99. So forget present-day accolades. Bowie was a pioneer; he played the game long before the NHL was formed in 1917. Bowie's significance today owes itself to the fact that he owns the best career goals-per-game average in any era of hockey.

During his 10-year career (from 1898 to 1908) he played 80 games and scored 234 goals—an average of almost three goals per game. It's unfair to evaluate stars of one era against another, but Bowie was clearly the Gretzky of his time. A lightweight of 112 pounds, he was a master stickhandler who scored multiple five-, six- and seven-goal games, and one eight-goal effort against the Montreal Shamrocks on January 16, 1907. In that season, Bowie scored 38 times in the 10-game schedule.

6.14 Pavol Demitra and Adam Oates. Ottawa rookie Pavol Demitra, playing in only his 26th NHL game, scored the last regular-season goal at venerable Boston Garden. Demitra's historic goal came at 12:11 of the third period in a 5-4 win over the Bruins on May 1, 1995. The last Bruin to score in the regular season was Cam Neely. Neely scored two minutes earlier (at 10:19 in the third period) on a feed from Adam Oates. The very last goal in the Garden's history was scored by Adam Oates May 14. Boston lost the game 3-2 to New Jersey and the quarterfinal playoff round 4-1. After 66 years of sport and entertainment, Boston Garden closed its famed doors for the last time.

6.15 Sandy Moger. The first goal scored at the Fleet Center was by Boston's Sandy Moger at 10:40 of the first period, October 7, 1995. In the game, Cam Neely scored the Fleet Center's first hat trick as Boston tied the New York Islanders 4-4.

6.16 29 power-play goals. Brett Hull is a power-play junkie. As of 1998-99, the Golden Brett has scored 214 times in man-advantage situations—a remarkable 37 per cent of his career-goal total of 584. His highest power-play season total is 29 goals, recorded twice (in 1990-91 and 1992-93).

6.17 Time: 1:18 Just 1:18 after stepping onto the ice for the first time in his NHL career, Lemieux scored his first NHL goal. It came on his first shift, on his first shot, October 11, 1984. Mario didn't notch another goal for 10 games. But he eventually got things going, winning top rookie honours in 1984-85 after scoring 43 times.

6.18 Phil Esposito. The NHL had never witnessed a performance like the Phil Esposito show of 1970-71, when he blasted home a record 76 goals on 550 shots. His 76-goal and 550-shot counts smashed Bobby Hull's mark of 58 goals on 414 shots in 1968-69.

6.19 Atlanta. The only time in NHL history a team from the United States moved to Canada was in 1980, when the Atlanta Flames replaced their flaming "A" with a flaming "C" and became the Calgary Flames. The Atlanta franchise joined the league in 1972-73, but although the Atlanta Flames remained competitive for eight seasons, they never won a playoff round. In May 1980, the team was sold to Vancouver businessman Nelson Skalbania and Calgary interests for a record U.S.$16 million. A year later Skalbania sold his 50 per cent share to local ownership to complete the deal.

6.20 413 shots. It doesn't take a rocket scientist to figure out which defenseman owns this record. Trailing super snipers Phil Esposito (550 and 426 shots in 1970-71 and 1971-72), Paul Kariya (429 shots in 1998-99) and Bobby Hull (414 shots in 1968-69) by just one shot on goal, Bobby Orr fired an astounding 413 shots in 1969-70, the most ever by an NHL defenseman. Orr scored 33 goals and 87 assists for 120 points to become the first and only defenseman to win the NHL scoring race. The next best shots-on-goal count by a D-man belongs to Ray Bourque, who had 390 shots in 1995-96.

GAME 6

HOCKEY CROSSWORD

(Solutions are on page 119)

Across

1. Montreal's No. 9, Maurice "___" ___

10. Team expected to lose

11. Top hockey player

12. ___ Simpson

13. Season before regular season

14. In midseason, teams ___ ___ the All-Star game

16. OHL's ___ Generals

19. Expelled or ___ out of the game

20. ___ Broten

23. What the announcer says at the start of a fight

25. Camera technique used to analyze a play

26. To study

27. 1960s and 70s Chicago's ___ ___

29. Peter and Anton ___

30. Shayne ___

Down

2. Veterans

3. 1980s Flyers sniper, Tim ___

4. Old-time goalie, Tiny ___

5. Gave or ___ a warning

6. 1972 Summit Series winner, Paul ___

7. Obey the ___ of the game.

8. 1987 rookie of the year, L.A.'s ___ ___

9. Consecutive games-played leader, he's an ___

15. Leg exercises

17. 1990s to playmaker ____ ____

18. Score a ____

21. 1960s Toronto old-timer, Jim ____

22. 1994 Rangers Cup-winner Brian ____

24. Clever

28. End ____ end

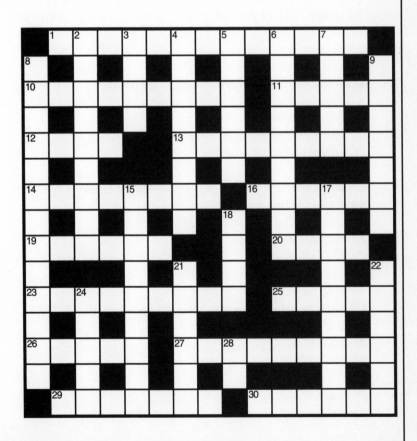

7

MILLENNIUM MEN

What was so special about the game in which Ron Francis recorded his 1,000th assist? Francis's millennium assist came on March 21, 1998, in a 4-3 win over Philadelphia. The victory was the Penguins' 1,000th in franchise history. Was it mere coincidence Francis scored his 1,000th assist in Pittsburgh's 1,000th win? Certainly, but the Pens were the 10th NHL club to win 1,000 games, and Francis wears No. 10. In this chapter we look at those special players and teams who have reached the 1,000 mark in assists, points, games and even goals.

(Answers are on page 87)

7.1 **Who was the first NHLer to score 1,000 points?**
A. Maurice Richard
B. Gordie Howe
C. Jean Béliveau
D. Bobby Hull

7.2 **Who was the first player from a post-1967 expansion team to hit the 1,000-point plateau?**
A. Los Angeles' Marcel Dionne
B. Philadelphia's Bobby Clarke
C. The Islanders' Bryan Trottier
D. Buffalo's Gilbert Perreault

7.3 **In which decade did an NHL team first produce two 1,000-point players in the same season?**
A. The 1960s
B. The 1970s
C. The 1980s
D. The 1990s

7.4   Which player took the longest time to record his 1,000th NHL point?
A. Henri Richard
B. Larry Murphy
C. Johnny Bucyk
D. Dale Hunter

7.5   Which NHL team in 1997-98 made hockey history, by icing three teammates who each reached the 1,000-point plateau in the same season?
A. The Washington Capitals
B. The New York Islanders
C. The Detroit Red Wings
D. The Edmonton Oilers

7.6   Which two 1,000-or-more-game NHLers with the same last name played in the exact same number of NHL games?
A. Maurice Richard and Henri Richard
B. Mike Murphy and Larry Murphy
C. Mike Ramsey and Craig Ramsey
D. Frank Mahovlich and Pete Mahovlich

7.7   After Joe Mullen, who is the second American-born player to score 1,000 points?
A. Brett Hull
B. Phil Housley
C. Chris Chelios
D. Pat LaFontaine

7.8   As of 1998-99, which 1,000-*game* NHLer has played with the most teams in his career?
A. Rob Ramage
B. Paul Coffey
C. Phil Housley
D. Larry Murphy

7.9 Which NHLer played on the most teams to reach his 1,000th point?
A. Larry Murphy
B. Brian Propp
C. Adam Oates
D. Phil Housley

7.10 As of 1998-99, who are the only father and son combination in NHL history to each score 1,000 points?
A. Syd and Gerry Abel
B. Gordie and Mark Howe
C. Bobby and Brett Hull
D. Ken and Ken Hodge, Jr.

7.11 As of 1998-99, how many European-trained players have reached the 1,000-*game* plateau in the NHL?
A. Only one, Borje Salming
B. Two players
C. Three players
D. Four players

7.12 Which 1,000-game NHLer scored the fewest goals in his career?
A. Doug Harvey
B. Harold Snepsts
C. Jay Wells
D. Brad Marsh

7.13 Who was the most recent NHLer to reach the 1,000-point mark with one team?
A. Boston's Ray Bourque
B. Detroit's Steve Yzerman
C. Pittsburgh's Mario Lemieux
D. Los Angeles' Dave Taylor

7.14 Who was the first European-trained NHLer to become a 1,000-point man?
A. Finland's Jari Kurri
B. Czechoslovakia's Peter Stastny
C. Yugoslavia's Ivan Boldirev
D. Finland's Tomas Sandstrom

7.15 Among the more than 50 NHLers with more than 1,000 career points, how many have scored 500 points with more than one NHL team?
A. Three players
B. Six players
C. Nine players
D. 12 players

MILLENIUM MEN
Answers

7.1 **B. Gordie Howe**
Howe became the NHL's first 1,000-point player on November 27, 1960. The historic marker came on an assist in a 2-0 win over Toronto. It was Howe's 938th game. Another eight years passed before Jean Béliveau recorded the league's second 1,000th point in March 1968. Maurice Richard, hockey's first 500-goal scorer, never reached the 1,000-point plateau.

7.2 **A. Los Angeles' Marcel Dionne**
Although Philadelphia's Bobby Clarke deserves credit for being the first member of a post-expansion club to hit 1,000 points with the same team, he could not catch Dionne, who reached the 1,000-point plateau first on January 7, 1981, just two months ahead of Clarke. Of course, Dionne's "first" is somewhat tarnished by the fact that 366 points of his 1,000-point total were scored with Detroit (an Original Six team) between 1971 and 1975. The remaining 634 points came with the Kings.

7.3   D. The 1990s

No team had two players score their 1,000th point in the same season until 1995-96, when Doug Gilmour and Larry Murphy each notched career point 1,000 with the Toronto Maple Leafs. Gilmour got his 1,000th point on December 23, 1995; Murphy on March 27, 1996. Each had played with multiple clubs before scoring their 1,000th point with the Maple Leafs.

7.4   D. Dale Hunter

No NHLer took more time to reach the millennium mark than Hunter. He recorded his 1,000th career point against Philadelphia in January 1998 during his 1,308th league game. "I knew this would come if I stuck around long enough," Hunter joked after Washington beat the Flyers 4-1. Hunter is also the most penalized 1,000-point man, with more than 3,500 penalty minutes.

1,000 Points in +1,000 Games*			
Player	**Team**	**Date**	**Game No.**
Dale Hunter	Washington	01/09/98	1,308
Larry Murphy	Toronto	03/27/96	1,228
Henri Richard	Montreal	12/20/73	1,194
Johnny Bucyk	Boston	11/09/72	1,144
Alex Delvecchio	Detroit	02/16/69	1,143
Norm Ullman	Detroit	10/16/71	1,113
Lanny McDonald	Calgary	03/07/89	1,101
*Current to 1997-98			

7.5   A. The Washington Capitals

When Washington does it, it goes all out. In 23 NHL seasons no NHLer had scored his 1,000th career point as a member of the Capitals. Then, in 1997-98, Phil Housley, Adam Oates and Dale Hunter each hit the 1,000-point milestone with Washington, the first 1,000-point trio from one team in league annals. Oates knocked home point number 1,000 on October 8, 1997; a month later, on November 8, 1997, Housley scored his 1,000th; Hunter made it a Washington hat trick on January 9, 1998. Washington's affinity for picking up veterans on the verge of their millennium point continued in 1998-99, when Brian Bellows scored career number 1,000 with the Caps.

7.6 C. Mike Ramsey and Craig Ramsey
As of 1998-99, the only two players with the same last name on the NHL's 1,000 games-played list are Mike and Craig Ramsey. They each played in Buffalo 14 seasons and totalled the exact same number of career games: 1,070 matches. Mike and Craig are not related other than by this amazing bit of trivia.

7.7 B. Phil Housley
The second 1,000-point American-born NHLer after Joe Mullen (who scored his on February 7, 1995) is Housley, from St. Paul, Minnesota. Housley hit the 1,000-point plateau in a 2-1 Capitals win against Edmonton, November 8, 1997.

7.8 A. Rob Ramage
A number of 1,000-game NHLers have played on six teams during their career. One of them, Paul Coffey, has suited up for seven (at last count). But as of 1998-99, Ramage is the most-travelled 1,000-game player, having signed with eight teams during 15 NHL seasons and 1,044 matches. Ramage's longest stay was in St. Louis (441 games); his shortest, in Montreal (14 games) and Philadelphia (15 games). His excursion through the league also took him to Colorado (234 games), Calgary (80), Toronto (160), Minnesota (34) and Tampa Bay (66).

7.9 D. Phil Housley
On November 8, 1997, Housley scored point number 1,000 playing for Washington, his sixth NHL team. Housley's career began in Buffalo in 1982-83, when he was chosen sixth overall by the Sabres. To reach point number 1,000, Housley scored 558 points with Buffalo, 259 points with Winnipeg, 22 points with St. Louis, 95 with Calgary, 16 with New Jersey and +50 with Washington. Housley is only the fifth defenseman to score 1,000 points in the NHL. Brian Propp, Adam Oates and Bernie Nicholls needed four clubs and Larry Murphy five clubs to get their millennium point.

7.10 C. Bobby and Brett Hull

The Hulls became the first father-son duo to net 1,000 points each on November 14, 1999, when Brett scored his 1,000th point by assisting on Jere Lehtinen's empty net goal against Boston. Brett became the 53rd NHLer to reach 1,000 points, almost 29 years after his dad, Bobby, became the league's fourth millennium man on December 12, 1970. Both Hulls scored number 1,000 on assists: Bobby in his 909th game and Brett in his 815th.

7.11 C. Three players

Only three Europeans have played 1,000 NHL games. Sweden's Borje Salming (1,148 games) was first in 1987-88, followed by Jari Kurri of Finland (1,251 games) in 1994-95 and Ulf Samuelsson of Sweden—who notched his 1,000th game on January 15, 1999. In 2000-01, Petr Svoboda of the Czech Republic should become the fourth Euro-NHLer to hit 1,000 games.

7.12 D. Brad Marsh

Brad Marsh meant much more to his teams than the scoring charts indicate. It was his defensive skills and leadership qualities that carried him through 1,086 NHL games. In his six-team, 15-year career, Marsh scored only 23 times—the lowest number of goals among all 1,000-game men.

The NHL's Lowest-Scoring 1,000-Game Players*				
Player	MPT†	Years	GP	Goals
Brad Marsh	Philadelphia	15	1,086	23
Terry Harper	Montreal	19	1,066	35
Dave Lewis	NYI	15	1,008	36
Craig Ludwig	Montreal	17	1,176	36
Harold Snepsts	Vancouver	17	1,033	38
Jean Guy Talbot	Montreal	17	1,056	43
Jay Wells	Los Angeles	18	1,098	47
Gordie Roberts	Minnesota	15	1,097	61

*Current to 1998-99
† MPT/Most prominent team

7.13 B. Detroit's Steve Yzerman

As of 1998-99, more than 50 players have reached the 1,000-point milestone, but less than half have done it on just one team. The most recent to hit 1,000 points on one team is Steve Yzerman, who recorded his 1,000th point on February 24, 1993, in his 10th season with the Red Wings. Since then almost 20 other players have scored 1,000 points, all while playing on multiple teams.

7.14 B. Czechoslovakia's Peter Stastny

As of 1998-99 only two European-trained players have hit the 1,000-point mark: Peter Stastny and Jari Kurri. Each began their NHL careers in 1980-81; Stastny with the Quebec Nordiques and Kurri in Edmonton as Wayne Gretzky's winger. Despite that difference, Stastny still potted his 1,000th faster, scoring the millennium marker on October 19, 1989. It came just 10 weeks ahead of Kurri's 1,000th—scored January 2, 1990.

7.15 A. Three players

As of 1997-98, only three NHLers have split their 1,000-point careers evenly between two teams. Some came very close though. Veterans such as Norm Ullman just missed, scoring 758 points for Detroit, 471 for Toronto. Dale Hunter almost did it too, with Quebec (458 points) and Washington (+500 points). Wayne Gretzky and Mark Messier were obvious choices in this category, but Ron Francis? Makes sense now that we told you!

500-Point Players on Multiple Teams*		
Player	**Team**	**Points**
Wayne Gretzky	Edmonton	1,669
	Los Angeles	918
Mark Messier	Edmonton	1,034
	New York	518
Ron Francis	Hartford/Carolina	873
	Pittsburgh	613
*Current to 1998-99		

GAME 7

THE 1,000-POINT PLAYERS

There are many ways to build a 1,000-point NHL career. Some snipers, such as Gilbert Perreault, have done it on one team; others have worn as many as five different jerseys before hitting the millennium milestone. In this game, match the players and the team with which they scored their 1,000th point.

(Solutions are on page 119)

Part 1

1. _____ Gordie Howe	A.	Buffalo Sabres
2. _____ Ray Bourque	B.	Minnesota North Stars
3. _____ Steve Larmer	C.	Pittsburgh Penguins
4. _____ Bobby Smith	D.	New Jersey Devils
5. _____ Dale Hawerchuk	E.	Detroit Red Wings
6. _____ Mario Lemieux	F.	New York Rangers
7. _____ Bernie Nicholls	G.	Los Angeles Kings
8. _____ Luc Robitaille	H.	Boston Bruins

Part 2

1. _____ Wayne Gretzky	A.	Washington Capitals
2. _____ Denis Potvin	B.	Calgary Flames
3. _____ Glenn Anderson	C.	Edmonton Oilers
4. _____ Michel Goulet	D.	Philadelphia Flyers
5. _____ Dale Hunter	E.	Chicago Blackhawks
6. _____ Lanny MacDonald	F.	Detroit Red Wings
7. _____ Darryl Sittler	G.	New York Islanders
8. _____ Steve Yzerman	H.	Toronto Maple Leafs

8

MANO A MANO

On February 19, 1944, Toronto's Jackie Hamilton was awarded a penalty shot after being pulled down by Bruins defenseman Dit Clapper. Referee Norm Lamport placed the puck at centre ice and Hamilton skated in, shot and scored on goalie Bert Gardiner. Clapper, the Boston captain, protested the goal, stating the puck had to be placed at the opposite blueline, not at centre ice (as was the rule then). Lamport yielded and signalled another penalty shot, this time to begin from the opposing blueline. Unruffled, Hamilton gathered up the puck from his blueline, confidently skated across the neutral zone toward the net, fired and scored again, becoming the only player to score twice on the same penalty shot. In this chapter, take your best shot, twice, and go mano a mano against these puck stoppers.

(Answers are on page 97)

8.1 What is the record for the fastest two goals by one player in regular-season action?
A. Three seconds
B. Four seconds
C. Five seconds
D. Six seconds

8.2 In February 1999 who said, "I don't want to go anywhere. Tell Bobby Clarke to shut his mouth. Just tell Bobby Clarke to leave me alone!"?
A. Chris Chelios
B. Tie Domi
C. Eric Lindros
D. Chris Gratton

8.3 Which former Toronto Maple Leaf captain boycotted the closing ceremonies of Maple Leaf Gardens in 1999?
A. George Armstrong
B. Ron Ellis
C. Darryl Sittler
D. Dave Keon

8.4 Which NHL All-Star defenseman became a head coach and trained his netminders with restraining straps and ropes?
A. Eddie Shore
B. Doug Harvey
C. Pierre Pilot
D. Bobby Orr

8.5 What *other* NHL milestone was reached during the Detroit-Colorado game in which Patrick Roy registered his 400th career win in February 1999?
A. Most career games played by a goalie (Patrick Roy)
B. Most career games played by a Russian (Igor Larionov)
C. Most career games played by a defenseman (Larry Murphy)
D. Most career games played by a captain (Joe Sakic)

8.6 What is the longest career of an NHLer who never scored a point?
A. 31 games
B. 41 games
C. 51 games
D. 61 games

8.7 Which Dallas Stars player hit his own coach, Ken Hitchcock, in the head with a puck during game action in February 1999?
A. Guy Carbonneau
B. Mike Modano
C. Mike Keane
D. Joe Nieuwendyk

8.8 Which Hockey Hall of Fame member became a Canadian senator in 1998?
A. Jean Béliveau
B. Frank Mahovlich
C. Guy Lafleur
D. Bobby Hull

8.9 In what decade were penalty shots first awarded to players against whom the foul was committed?
A. The 1930s
B. The 1940s
C. The 1950s
D. The 1960s

8.10 In 1998-99, what hockey first did Vince Riendeau accomplish?
A. Riendeau was the first North American to play in a Russian hockey league
B. Riendeau was the first NHLer from North America to play in a Russian hockey league
C. Riendeau was the first North American to play in a Swedish hockey league
D. Riendeau was the first NHLer from North America to play in a Swedish hockey league

8.11 What percentage of players in 1998-99 wore visors?
A. 5 per cent
B. 15 per cent
C. 25 per cent
D. 35 per cent

8.12 Who are Paul and Greg Devorski?
A. Brothers who are NHL player agents
B. Brothers who are NHL on-ice officials
C. Brothers who are NHL team physicians
D. Brothers who are NHL Zamboni drivers

8.13 In what year did the first American collegiate player jump directly to the NHL?
A. 1928
B. 1948
C. 1968
D. 1988

8.14 Which NHL arena has the most expensive concession prices?
A. The United Center in Chicago
B. The Arrowhead Pond of Anaheim
C. The Air Canada Centre in Toronto
D. The Keil Center in St. Louis

8.15 Who was the first European-trained player to captain an NHL team?
A. Chicago's Stan Mikita
B. Winnipeg's Lars-Erik Sjoberg
C. Quebec's Peter Stastny
D. Toronto's Mats Sundin

8.16 What is the highest number of times one NHLer has led or shared the lead in fighting majors?
A. No player has ever done it twice
B. Two times
C. Three times
D. Four times

8.17 How much money did Philadelphia general manager Bobby Clarke pay centre Chris Gratton in 1997-98 (Gratton's only complete season with the Flyers)?
A. $4 million
B. $6 million
C. $8 million
D. $10 million

8.18 Which Original Six arena was the first to have a four-sided clock, the first to use Herculite glass and the first to install separate penalty boxes?
A. Maple Leaf Gardens
B. The Detroit Olympia
C. The Montreal Forum
D. Madison Square Garden

8.19 What kind of injury forced Mark Messier to miss his first game since joining Vancouver in 1997?
A. A groin pull
B. A concussion
C. A separated shoulder
D. A broken finger

MANO A MANO
Answers

8.1 B. Four seconds
It's hard to imagine scoring two goals faster than four seconds apart. Consider how much clock time it takes after scoring the first goal to win the face-off, skate, maybe take a pass, shoot and score again. But it's happened twice, almost 64 years apart. The Montreal Maroons' Nels Stewart scored two goals in four seconds at 8:24 and 8:28 of the third period on January 3, 1931, in a 5-3 win. More recently, on December 15, 1995, Winnipeg's Deron Quint scored at 7:51 and 7:55 of the second period as the Jets defeated the Oilers 9-4.

8.2 A. Chris Chelios
Responding to reports that he would be traded to the Flyers, Chelios said, "I've heard I'm going to Philly for Dainius Zubrus and I know that's not going to happen. That's not enough. Maybe if it was for Eric Lindros, I would believe it. " The long-time Chicago D-man then blasted Clarke: "I don't want to go anywhere. Tell Bobby Clarke to shut his mouth. Just tell Bobby Clarke to leave me alone!" Despite the denials, Chelios was

soon dealt: not to Clarke's Flyers, but to Chicago's archrival, the Detroit Red Wings.

8.3 D. Dave Keon

More than 100 former Leaf players and coaches participated in the closing ceremonies of Maple Leaf Gardens, but not Keon, whose bitter falling out with the late owner Harold Ballard and, later, Darryl Sittler (who took over the Leafs captaincy from Keon), seemed to be at the root of his 24-year estrangement from the franchise. Some say that Keon was considering attending but changed his mind after receiving a form letter invitation, which began, "Dear Former Player." Keon deserved better. He played 1,062 games with Toronto and scored 365 goals and 493 assists; won the Calder Trophy as the NHL top rookie, two Lady Byng Trophies as most gentlemanly player, plus four Stanley Cups and the Conn Smythe as playoff MVP in 1967—the last time the club won the Cup. (Four other important Leaf players missed the game for various reasons: Ted Kennedy, Bert Olmstead, Andy Bathgate and Paul Henderson.)

8.4 A. Eddie Shore

Few old-time goaltenders received training or advice from their coaches. Much like their rudimentary equipment (which, for the most part, they invented and refined themselves), the original backstoppers were self-taught; skills were honed without formal instruction but through basic practice and game experience. The exception to the rule might be Eddie Shore, the NHL's greatest defenseman of the 1920s and 1930s. When Shore retired he bought and coached the Springfield Indians of the AHL. He had many tricks to keep his goalies on their feet and in the net. At practice he tied a belt around a goalie's neck and another around his knees to prevent him from either going down or allowing the puck through his legs. At other times he put a bar between the posts and a leash on his netminders to prevent them from backing into the net or wandering out too far. Shore's diabolical ways destroyed many players, who quit hockey rather than play for him. Others called him a "masterful teacher," and credited his instruction with making them into stars.

8.5 C. Most career games played by a defenseman (Larry Murphy)
As with most games between Detroit and Colorado, the night of February 5, 1999, held a special meaning for both clubs and, in particular, Patrick Roy and Larry Murphy. Roy, after a miserable season start, was on a 10-game tear, looking to become only the fifth goalie in league history to record 400 wins. Murphy, who had missed just 26 games in 19 seasons and had been sidelined the previous game, was on the verge of becoming the all-time leader for career games among defensemen. That afternoon Murphy received medical clearance to play and the All-Star blueliner recorded the 1,447th game of his career, smashing Tim Horton's league record for games played by a D-man. Roy got win number 400, too. Roy allowed one goal and then shut the door on the Red Wings in the 3-1 win. It was Colorado's 11th straight victory, the longest streak in the NHL since 1993.

8.6 D. 61 games
The longest career without scoring a point belongs to Detroit defenseman Gord Strate, who played 61 games during his entire career and never registered a point in three seasons. In fact, most of the 13 NHLers who have played 20 or more games without scoring a point are rearguards, with skills just below NHL calibre. In the 1990s, the longest pointless streak belongs to Gord Kruppke, another Detroit blueliner who played 23 games without a point between 1990-91 and 1993-94.

The Longest Career Scoring Droughts			
Player	Team	Seasons	GP
Gord Strate	Detroit	1956 to 1959	61
Frank Peters	NYR	1930-31	43
Billy Cameron	Mtl.-NYA	1923 to 1925	39
Patsy Callighen	NYR	1927-28	36
Stephane Guerard	Quebec	1987 to 1990	34
(six other pointless players—not listed)			
Gord Kruppke	Detroit	1990 to 1994	23
Barry Boughner	Oak-Calif.	1969 to 1971	20

8.7 C. Mike Keane
On February 15, 1999, Dallas coach Ken Hitchcock received 16 stitches after being struck in the head by a clearing shot from Mike Keane. At the time, Hitchcock was admonishing a player for making a blunder. Asked about Keane, Hitchcock replied, "We've asked him to make sure and check into condos in Tampa and see how he likes it there." Mike Modano noted, "Now he knows what it feels like to be a hockey player."

8.8 B. Frank Mahovlich
Mahovlich, the star winger of Toronto and Montreal in the 1960s and 1970s, entered a whole new arena in 1998 after being appointed by Canadian Prime Minister Jean Chretien to the Canadian Senate. Although a few hockey players have been elected to Canada's House of Commons, the Big M is the first senator. The prime minister picked Mahovlich because "it was a way to recognize all the hockey players who make a great contribution, not only in the so-called entertainment of hockey but in their private life." Mahovlich's senatorial salary is $65,000, plus almost $20,000 a year for expenses. After 17 years in the NHL, his pension from the league is just $13,000 annually.

8.9 D. The 1960s
There have been many changes in penalty-shot rules since they were first introduced by the NHL in 1934. Perhaps the most important change came in 1961-62, when the NHL ruled that the fouled player was awarded the penalty shot. Prior to that date the fouled team could appoint anyone to take the shot. One unusual case occurred on November 8, 1959, when the old rule was unwittingly reversed by referee Dalton McArthur. McArthur permitted the team *who caused the foul* to appoint the opposing shooter *instead* of allowing the fouled team to choose. The penalty shot was awarded after Boston forward Bronco Horvath was fouled on a breakaway by Chicago's Al Arbour. Since it was only the tenth penalty-shot call in 10 years, McArthur became confused and allowed Chicago to choose instead of the Bruins. Despite Boston's protests, the Hawks selected little-used Bruin Larry Leach to take the shot on

Glenn Hall. Leach failed to score and Horvath, who was running a 22-game scoring streak, ended up missing the league scoring title that season by just one point.

8.10 B. Riendeau was the first NHLer from North America to play in a Russian hockey league

Riendeau, who played 184 games in eight NHL seasons with Montreal, St. Louis, Detroit and Boston, made hockey history in February 1999 when he became the first former NHLer (from outside Russia) to join the Russian Hockey League. Riendeau backstopped for Lada Togliatti, a club based in the industrial city of Togliatti, 700 kilometres southeast of Moscow. Although Riendeau could be playing elsewhere in Europe, he chose Russia because, "I'm not your typical type of guy. This is a chance to deal with a new culture, a new language. To me, this is life, trying new things," said Riendeau in a *National Post* story. Riendeau's first on-ice experience was positive. After back-to-back victories in the nets his teammates all came up to him. "I've no idea what they were saying, but they seemed happy," said Riendeau. In 1990 Todd Hartje became the first North American to play in Russia, but Hartje never made it to the NHL.

8.11 B. 15 percent

Only 89 players—or 14.9 per cent—wore visors during the 1998-99 season. Montreal and Ottawa each iced seven players sporting face shields, the most among NHL clubs. Three teams (Edmonton, Chicago and San Jose) had no players wearing eye protection.

8.12 B. Brothers who are NHL on-ice officials

The Devorskis are the first brothers to officiate in the NHL. Paul, 11 years Greg's senior, has been refereeing since 1989; his brother, a linesman, since 1993. Because of their age difference, the brothers had little in common as siblings, except hockey. Today, they still share their love of the game, as officials. "Once we're out there, we're two guys with jobs to do, and we're more concerned about not screwing up [than with what the other one is doing]." Their first game together, during Greg's first week on the job, came in October 1993 in Detroit, between the Red Wings and Winnipeg. Although the Devorskis both work about 70 games per season, they are teamed for no more than five or six games.

8.13 A. 1928
Few hockey people know the name Myles Lane, but when Lane played for Dartmouth during the 1920s he was unequalled on the ice, diamond and gridiron, and earned letters in all three team sports and all-American status in 1927. In hockey, Lane set school records for most goals by a defenseman (20 goals in 1925-26). After graduating from Dartmouth in 1928, he joined the New York Rangers, becoming the first American collegiate player to go directly to the NHL. The following season, 1928-29, he won a Stanley Cup with Boston. Lane was enshrined in the United States Hockey Hall of Fame in 1973.

8.14 A. The United Center in Chicago
In a 1998 study of 94 professional venues, Street and Smith's *Sports Business Journal* found that the highest prices for concessions are at Chicago's United Center. By comparison, sports fans still fork out more for beer and dogs if they take in a ball game at Boston's Fenway Park, which ranked first overall in the analysis. Among NHL arenas, the highest prices for beer were in Phoenix and New Jersey ($4.50/14 ounces); the least expensive suds, at the old Maple Leaf Gardens ($1.63/14 ounces). St. Louis' Kiel Center charged the steepest price for soda ($2.25/12 ounces), while the cheapest hot dog could be had in Calgary ($1.63).

8.15 B. Winnipeg's Lars-Erik Sjoberg
Before the Winnipeg Jets crashed, burned and resurrected in the desert as the Phoenix Coyotes, they, more than any other team, developed the first European-North American link in hockey. Sjoberg, already a 30-year-old veteran Swedish defenseman, was among the first Europeans attracted by Winnipeg. Sjoberg played six seasons with the Jets: his first five in the WHA and his last, 1979-80, as an NHLer when the two leagues merged. Sjoberb's experience on European ice prepared him well for

North American play. He became the Jets' captain in 1975, leading the team to three Avco World Trophies in four years. When Winnipeg became an NHL franchise in 1979 Sjoberg wore the "C," becoming the league's first European-trained captain.

8.16 D. Four times

Many celebrated fighters, including Mike Peluso, Dave Schultz and Tiger Williams, have totalled more penalty minutes and more fighting majors than 1960s tough guy Reggie Fleming. But Fleming is the only NHL brawler to lead or share the lead in fighting majors four times. In his 1960-61 rookie season Fleming established his credentials, matching veteran fighters Lou Fontinato and Bert Olmstead with five fighting majors. He shared the lead three more times in the 1960s with four fights in 1964-65, five in 1965-66 and eight in 1966-67. His sparring skills were matched only by the likes of enforcers John Ferguson and Ted Green.

8.17 D. $10 million

In 1997, Philadelphia general manager Bobby Clarke really liked what he saw in Tampa Bay's six-foot-four, 218-pound centre Chris Gratton. Could he be another John LeClair? He signed Gratton to a five-year offer worth $16.5 million (which Tampa didn't match), $10 million of which was front-loaded in the first year. But after one season, Gratton failed to impress Clarke, who sent him back to the Lightning for the same player he gave up originally, Mikael Renberg. Clarke's self-admitted mistake was huge. By trading away Renberg, he broke up the Flyers' most productive scoring unit, the Legion of Doom, and, ultimately, cost the Flyers $10 million (which Gratton received in his only season as a Flyer). The big centre scored 62 points in Philly in 1997-98, or $161,290.32 per point.

8.18 A. Maple Leaf Gardens

When the Gardens closed its doors to hockey on February 13, 1999, it signalled the end of an era: the last of the Original Six buildings. Each of the six rinks—Madison Square Garden, the Detroit Olympia, the Montreal Forum, Boston Garden,

Chicago Stadium and the Gardens—were as unique in character and history as the teams that called them home. But MLG might be a little more special: it was the first hockey building with a four-sided clock (1932), Herculite glass (1947), escalators (1955) and separate penalty boxes (1962).

8.19 B. A concussion

The crash into the goal net was spectacular. Messier, on his second shift of a game against Calgary, December 22, 1998, smashed into the Flames' net in full flight, snapping his head back on one of the posts before slamming down on the ice. The impact sent a chill through the crowd. Messier, who scored on the play, was taken to the dressing room and didn't return. The next night he missed his first game since joining Vancouver—a streak of 113 consecutive contests. The concussion was listed as day-to-day.

GAME 8
TEAM GUNNERS

As of 1998-99, only one NHLer led more than one team for most goals scored in a season. Is it Wayne Gretzky? Alexander Mogilny? Brett Hull? No other sniper can equal Teemu Selanne, who holds the best totals with two clubs, the Phoenix Coyotes/Winnipeg Jets (76 goals) and the Mighty Ducks of Anaheim (52 goals). In this game, match the team and the players who hold their clubs' records for most goals scored in one season.

(Solutions are on page 120)

1. _____	Boston Bruins	A.	Brett Hull
2. _____	Buffalo Sabres	B.	Alexei Yashin
3. _____	Calgary Flames	C.	Phil Esposito
4. _____	Chicago Blackhawks	D.	Mario Lemieux
5. _____	Colorado Avalanche	E.	Lanny McDonald
6. _____	Detroit Red Wings	F.	Pavel Bure
7. _____	Edmonton Oilers	G.	Steve Yzerman
8. _____	Montreal Canadiens	H.	Michel Goulet
9. _____	New York Rangers	I.	Alexander Mogilny
10. _____	Ottawa Senators	J.	Dennis Maruk
11. _____	Philadelphia Flyers	K.	Wayne Gretzky
12. _____	Pittsburgh Penguins	L.	Bobby Hull
13. _____	St. Louis Blues	M.	Adam Graves
14. _____	Toronto Maple Leafs	N.	Reggie Leach
15. _____	Vancouver Canucks	O.	Rick Vaive
16. _____	Washington Capitals	P.	Guy Lafleur

9

SILVERADO

Many roads lead to the Stanley Cup; many more turn into dead ends. Defenseman Gerry Hart knows that better than anyone. Hart, an inaugural member of the New York Islanders in 1972-73, played seven seasons with the club before being claimed by Quebec in the 1979 NHL Expansion Draft. The Islanders went on to win four straight Stanley Cups, beginning in 1980. In this final chapter, we search for that mythical arena of Stanley Cup fame, Silverado. Don't get lost out there on the highway.

(Answers are on page 110)

9.1 **Which NHLer won the most Stanley Cups in the 1990s?**
A. Mario Lemieux
B. Larry Murphy
C. Patrick Roy
D. Claude Lemieux

9.2 **Which team sported the first Swedish-trained player to win the Stanley Cup?**
A. The Boston Bruins in 1971-72
B. The Montreal Canadiens in 1978-79
C. The New York Islanders in 1979-80
D. The Edmonton Oilers in 1983-84

9.3 **Which team has won the Stanley Cup most often in overtime action in the last playoff game?**
A. The Toronto Maple Leafs
B. The Detroit Red Wings
C. The Montreal Canadiens
D. The Philadelphia Flyers

9.4 After Scotty Bowman and Toe Blake, which NHL coach won the most Stanley Cups?
A. Toronto's Punch Imlach
B. Edmonton's Glen Sather
C. The Islanders' Al Arbour
D. Toronto's Hap Day

9.5 In a 1923 Stanley Cup final game Ottawa Senators goalie Clint Benedict told his defenseman, King Clancy, "Here, kid. Take care of this place 'till I get back." Where was "this place"?
A. The goal net
B. The penalty box
C. The trainer's massage table
D. A bar stool in the lounge car on a train

9.6 As of 1998, what is the most number of shots faced by an NHL goalie in one playoff season?
A. Between 500 and 600 shots
B. Between 600 and 700 shots
C. Between 700 and 800 shots
D. More than 800 shots

9.7 What is the most number of goals allowed by a goaltender in a best-of-seven Stanley Cup final series?
A. Between 20 and 25 goals
B. Between 25 and 30 goals
C. Between 30 and 35 goals
D. More than 35 goals

9.8 In the notorious incident during the 1989 playoffs, where Ron Hextall attacked Chris Chelios with his blocker, which Flyer was Hextall defending?
A. Tim Kerr
B. Pelle Eklund
C. Brian Propp
D. Mark Howe

9.9 As of 1999, who is the greatest scorer *never* to win the Stanley Cup?
A. Marcel Dionne
B. Ray Bourque
C. Mike Gartner
D. Dale Hawerchuk

9.10 Which team iced the first Czech-trained player to win the Stanley Cup?
A. The New York Islanders in 1979-80
B. The Edmonton Oilers in 1983-84
C. The Calgary Flames in 1988-89
D. The Pittsburgh Penguins in 1990-91

9.11. What kind of bet did U.S. President Bill Clinton and Canadian Prime Minister Jean Chretien make on the outcome of the 1998 Eastern Conference semifinal between the Washington Capitals and the Ottawa Senators?
A. The loser hosts dinner for the winning team
B. The loser wears the winning team's hockey sweater
C. The loser makes a $1,000 contribution to the winner's favourite charity
D. The loser sings the winner's national anthem at the next Ottawa-Washington game

9.12 Which country produced the first players to win the World Championships, the Olympics and the Stanley Cup?
A. Canada
B. United States
C. Russia
D. Sweden

9.13 Since Toronto and Montreal met in the Stanley Cup finals in 1967, how many other all-Canadian finals have occurred?
A. None
B. Only one Cup final
C. Two Cup finals
D. Three Cup finals

9.14 Which goalie has the best career-winning percentage in Stanley Cup finals history (minimum 15 games)?
A. Montreal's Ken Dryden
B. The Islanders' Billy Smith
C. Edmonton's Grant Fuhr
D. Colorado's Patrick Roy

9.15 What is the average number of shots faced by Stanley Cup-winning goalie tandems in one playoff year since 1983?
A. Between 400 and 500 shots
B. Between 500 and 600 shots
C. Between 600 and 700 shots
D. More than 700 shots

9.16 Who was the last active member of the Edmonton Oilers' Stanley Cup dynasty teams?
A. Kevin Lowe
B. Craig MacTavish
C. Kelly Buchberger
D. Bill Ranford

9.17 After Wayne Gretzky, who scored the most game-winning playoff goals?
A. Maurice Richard
B. Mario Lemieux
C. Mike Bossy
D. Claude Lemieux

9.18 As of 1997-98, how many of Wayne Gretzky's record 122 career playoff goals were game winners?
A. 20 of 122 goals
B. 24 of 122 goals
C. 28 of 122 goals
D. 32 of 122 goals

SILVERADO
Answers

9.1 B. Larry Murphy

As of 1998, Murphy had won four Stanley Cups in the 1990s, the most among all NHLers. A freewheeling defenseman, Murphy broke into the NHL in 1981-82 and set the record for rookie D-men with 60 assists and 76 points. It took four teams and 10 more years before he finally became a Stanley Cup champion with the 1991 and 1992 Pittsburgh Penguins. Traded to his hometown of Toronto in 1995, Murphy played a sound defensive game, but his numbers slumped along with the fortunes of the Maple Leafs. Highly paid, he became a target for angry fans and the media. His trade to Detroit for future considerations in 1997 brought widespread skepticism, but Murphy silenced his critics and became half of the Red Wings' top defense duo with Nicklas Lidstrom. He was a key contributor to Detroit championships in 1997 and 1998, bringing his total to four Stanley Cups in the 1990s.

9.2 C. The New York Islanders in 1979-80

When the Islanders began building their dynasty team of the 1980s, they had two Swedish role players in the lineup: defenseman Stephan Persson and right-winger Anders Kallur. Persson, a Swedish national team member, was selected late in the 1974 draft and began playing for New York in 1977-78. Kallar signed as a free agent in 1979 after being named Swedish player of the year. Both contributed to all four Islander championships. They are the first Swedes in NHL history to win the Stanley Cup.

9.3 C. The Montreal Canadiens

Since its inaugural season in 1917-18, the NHL has seen 13 Stanley Cup champions declared in overtime. Considering Montreal has won 24 championships during its history, it's a safe bet that the Habs would also lead in Cup-deciding overtime games. The Canadiens played in six sudden-death matches, winning four Cups (1944, 1953, 1966 and 1977) and losing two (1951 and 1954) in overtime decisions.

9.4   D. Toronto's Hap Day

As of 1999, Bowman and Blake have each won a record eight Stanley Cups. The next-highest number of Cup victories by a coach belongs to Hap Day, who in his 10-year career as bench boss of the Maple Leafs won five championships between 1940-41 and 1949-50. Day began his NHL career as a player. He was Toronto's first team captain, anchoring the blueline with Red Horner and King Clancy. In 1929, he notched a four-goal game to tie an NHL record for defensemen. As a bench boss, Day had a highlight-reel career. He coached the Leafs to the greatest comeback in league history; the team rebounded from a 0-3 deficit to win 1942's championship. Five years later Day began a string of three straight Stanley Cups, a first for an NHL coach. Day also officiated at the NHL level and served as the Leafs' assistant general manager under Conn Smythe. Day was elected to the Hockey Hall of Fame in 1961.

9.5   A. The goal net

Clancy is the only NHLer to play every position—including goalie—in one Stanley Cup game. In Game 2 of the 1923 Ottawa-Edmonton Cup finals, Clancy, a second-year D-man, subbed for Ottawa's injured defensive stars George Boucher and Eddie Gerard, winded centre Frank Nighbor, bruised left-winger Cy Denneny and exhausted right-winger Punch Broadbent. With only 10 minutes remaining in the game, Senators goalie Benedict drew a penalty and was forced to serve it in the box, as was the custom in old-time hockey. Out skated Clancy again, met by Benedict, who passed on his stick and the famous line about taking care of "this place."

9.6   D. More than 800 shots

Since shots faced by goaltenders became an official statistic in 1982-83, a few interesting trivia facts have come to light. As of 1998, for example, the highest shots-against count in the play-offs is owned by a losing goalie. In fact, the top three spots are filled by netminders who succeeded in reaching the finals but lost the Cup. Vancouver's Kirk McLean ranked first in the rubber parade, facing a record 820 shots on net in 24 playoff games in 1994. Of the top 10, Felix Potvin of Toronto was the only goalie who failed to make the finals, losing a heartbreaking semifinal round to Los Angeles in 1993.

Most Shots Faced in the Playoffs*					
Player	Team	Year	GP	SA[†]	SAPG[†]
Kirk McLean	Vancouver	1994	24	820	31.9
Ron Hextall	Philadelphia	1987	26	769	30.0
J. Vanbiesbrouck	Florida	1996	22	735	33.1
Bill Ranford	Edmonton	1990	22	672	28.8
Kelly Hrudey	Los Angeles	1993	20	656	31.2
Patrick Roy	Colorado	1996	22	649	26.8
Patrick Roy	Montreal	1993	20	647	30.0
Felix Potvin	Toronto	1993	21	636	29.2
Tom Barrasso	Pittsburgh	1991	20	629	32.1
Mike Richter	New York	1994	23	623	26.4

*Current to 1998
[†] SA/Shots against, SAPG/Shots against per game

9.7 C. Between 30 and 35 goals
Peppered by Montreal's offensive juggernaut of Yvan Cournoyer, Jacques Lemaire and the Mahovlich brothers, Chicago's Tony Esposito gave up a record 33 goals in six games as the Canadiens won the best-of-seven series 4-2, outscoring the Hawks 33-23.

9.8 C. Brian Propp
During the 1989 playoffs Hextall lost it, mugging Chelios with his blocker after the Chicago rearguard elbowed Brian Propp into unconsciousness. Later, Propp called Chelios "a lousy person." Chelios responded with, "He's [Propp] a gutless jerk." Hextall earned a 12-game suspension for the assault; Chelios took home his first Norris Trophy as the league's most outstanding defenseman.

9.9 A. Marcel Dionne
The only two NHLers among the top 10 all-time scorers without Stanley Cups are Marcel Dionne and Ray Bourque. Dionne,

behind only Wayne Gretzky and Gordie Howe, with 1,771 points, never got closer to the Cup than the quarterfinals in 18 seasons with Detroit, Los Angeles and the New York Rangers. On nine occasions Dionne's teams never made it past the regular season. Bourque, with more than 1,400 points, has gone to the Cup finals twice, losing to Edmonton in 1988 and 1990.

9.10 B. The Edmonton Oilers in 1983-84

The first Czech-trained NHLer to win the Stanley Cup is Jaroslav Pouzar. Selected in the fourth round (83rd overall) by the Oilers in the 1982 draft, Pouzar, age 30, was already a Czech veteran of six world championship tournaments and two Olympics when he joined Edmonton for the 1982-83 season. His NHL entrance was a classic case of joining the right team at the right time. He won his first Stanley Cup the following year, 1983-84, and two more Oiler Cups before heading back to Europe in 1987. Pouzar won three Stanley Cups and played only 186 NHL regular-season games. (Another Czech player who hit the NHL jackpot was Jiri Hrdina. Hrdina played just four complete seasons, but during that time he won the Stanley Cup with the 1989 Calgary Flames in his first year and two more Cups in his third and fourth years with the 1991 and 1992 Pittsburgh Penguins. Hrdina won three Cups on two different teams and played in just 250 NHL games!)

9.11 B. The loser wears the winning team's hockey sweater

After Washington beat Ottawa 4-1 in 1998's semifinals, Clinton clinched the bet between the two nation's leaders and provided Chretien with the Capitals' blue-black-and-white sweater to wear in public. The Canadian prime minister donned the Caps sweater in front of cameras in England, where world leaders of the G8 were meeting. Clinton and Chretien also exchanged hockey sticks.

9.12 D. Sweden

The first players to win World, Olympic and Stanley Cup championships in separate tournaments were Swedes Tomas

Jonsson, Mats Naslund and Hakan Loob. Each captured the World title with Sweden in 1991, an Olympic gold medal in 1994 and, on different occasions with different teams, the Stanley Cup (Jonsson in 1982 and 1983 with the Islanders, Naslund in 1986 with Montreal and Loob with Calgary in 1989).

9.13 C. Two Cup finals
Since Toronto downed Montreal to win the Stanley Cup in 1967, only two other finals series in more than 30 years were entirely Canadian affairs: both the 1986 and 1989 Cup finals pitted Calgary against Montreal, with each team winning one championship.

9.14 A. Montreal's Ken Dryden
Dryden's all-too-brief career spanned just eight seasons, but he made every one of them count: he won six Stanley Cups with Montreal between 1971 and 1979. The Canadiens captured the Cup every time they reached the final round. Dryden played in every game for a record 24 wins and eight losses for a .750 winning percentage, the best in finals history.

9.15 B. Between 500 and 600 shots
From 1983-84 to 1997-98, the Stanley Cup was won by 15 goaltending tandems, averaging 592 shots to win the championship. The toughest year was 1990-91, when Pittsburgh's Tom Barrasso (629 shots) and Frank Pietrangelo (148 shots) combined for 777 shots allowed. In 24 games the pair gave up 51 goals as the Penguins won their first Cup. In 1987-88, Grant Fuhr of the Edmonton Oilers played all 19 games, allowing 55 goals on 471 shots, the least number of shots faced by a Cup-winning goalie since these stats became official in the early 1980s.

9.16 C. Kelly Buchberger
At the start of 1997-98, Buchberger and Lowe were the only remaining members from the Oilers' championship era. Lowe, a five-time Cup winner with Edmonton, played just five games in 1997-98 before ending his 19-year career to become an assistant coach. Buchberger, who won two Oiler Cups in 1987 and

1990, remained the team's only player from that dynasty era still active into 1999.

9.17 D. Claude Lemieux

No matter how much criticism Lemieux attracts for his subpar offensive numbers during the regular season, all is forgotten come playoff time. In the postseason, he is a model of consistency. Lemieux's 19 postseason game winners is second only to Gretzky's tally, and surprisingly ahead of the numbers held by more conspicuous playoff heroes, including Maurice Richard (18), Mike Bossy (17) and Glenn Anderson (17).

9.18 B. 24 of 122 goals

The Great One holds both the record for most career playoff goals (122) and most game winners (24) in postseason. On average, Gretzky decided a postseason match with every fifth goal he scored!

Most Game-Winning Goals in the Playoffs (Career)*

Player	Team	Goals
Wayne Gretzky	Edm, LA, St.L, NYR	24
Claude Lemieux	Mtl, NJ, Col	19
Maurice Richard	Mtl	18
Mike Bossy	NYI	17
Glenn Anderson	Edm, Tor, NYR, St.L	17
Jean Béliveau	Mtl	15
Yvan Cournoyer	Mtl	15

Current to 1997-98

SOLUTIONS TO GAMES

Game 1: GRETZKY'S OFFICE

1.	Sin Bin	J.	The penalty box
2.	Cage	H.	The net
3.	Brouhaha	C.	A fight
4.	Bench boss	F.	The coach
5.	Biscuit	A.	The puck
6.	A box	O.	Defensive formation while short-handed
7.	Gretzky's office	B.	Behind the net
8.	Goon	K.	A fighter
9.	Mucker	N.	A grinder
10.	Paddle	M.	A goalie stick
11.	Pipes	D.	The goalposts
12.	Riding the pines	G.	The player's bench
13.	Spin-a-rama	I.	A 360-degree turn
14.	Zebra	E.	An on-ice official
15.	Top shelf	L.	Upper part of net

Game 2: THE AGE OF EXPANSION

The remaining letters are in white-on-black lettering. In descending order they spell our hidden phrase: N-A-T-I-O-N-A-L H-O-C-K-E-Y L-E-A-G-U-E E-X-P-A-N-S-I-O-N.

Game 3: HOCKEY ROCKS

Part 1

1.	"Big League"	F.	Tom Cochrane
2.	"Gretzky Rocks"	D.	The Pursuit of Happiness
3.	"He Looked a Lot Like Tiger Williams"	G.	The Hanson Brothers
4.	"The Hockey Song"	A.	Stompin' Tom Connors
5.	"Fifty-Mission Cap"	C.	The Tragically Hip
6.	"Hockey"	B.	Jane Siberry
7.	"Clear the Track, Here Comes Shack"	E.	The Secrets

Part 2

1.	_____ "Rock 'em Sock 'em Techno"	B.	Don Cherry with BKS
2.	_____ "Pandemonium"	F.	Tommy Hunter
3.	_____ "The Ballad of Wendel Clark"	G.	The Rheostatics
4.	_____ "Raised on Robbery"	A.	Joni Mitchell
5.	_____ "Signin' with the NHL"	E.	Bruno Gerussi
6.	_____ "Overtime"	C.	DOA
7.	_____ The *Hockey Night in Canada* theme	D.	Shuffle Demons

Game 4: THE LUCKY 13

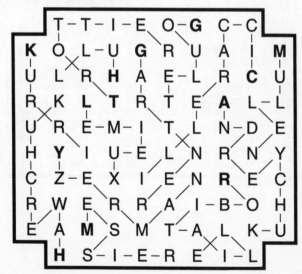

117

Game 5: TWIN PEAKS

Among the 17 NHLers to win both the Hart and Art Ross in a single season, the only blueliner is BOBBY ORR. The letters of his name are in white-on-black lettering and spelled in descending order. The other 16 double-award winners are:

Mario Lemieux	Brian Trottier	Bill Cowley
Wayne Gretzky	Elmer Lach	Max Bentley
Nels Stewart	Bernie Geoffrion	Guy Lafleur
Jean Béliveau	Howie Morenz	Toe Blake
Bobby Hull	Stan Mikita	Gordie Howe
Phil Esposito		

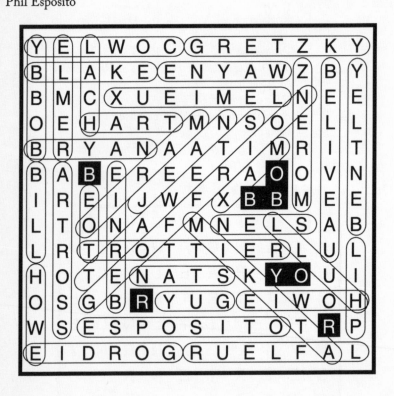

Game 6: HOCKEY CROSSWORD

Game 7: THE 1,000-POINT PLAYERS

Part 1

1. Gordie Howe	E. Detroit Red Wings
2. Ray Bourque	H. Boston Bruins
3. Steve Larmer	F. New York Rangers
4. Bobby Smith	B. Minnesota North Stars
5. Dale Hawerchuk	A. Buffalo Sabres
6. Mario Lemieux	C. Pittsburgh Penguins
7. Bernie Nicholls	D. New Jersey Devils
8. Luc Robitaille	G. Los Angeles Kings

Part 2

1. Wayne Gretzky	C. Edmonton Oilers
2. Denis Potvin	G. New York Islanders
3. Glenn Anderson	H. Toronto Maple Leafs
4. Michel Goulet	E. Chicago Blackhawks
5. Dale Hunter	A. Washington Capitals
6. Lanny MacDonald	B. Calgary Flames
7. Darryl Sittler	D. Philadelphia Flyers
8. Steve Yzerman	F. Detroit Red Wings

Game 8: TEAM GUNNERS

1.	Boston	C.	Phil Esposito	76 goals — 1970-71
2.	Buffalo	I.	Alex Mogilny	76 goals — 1992-93
3.	Calgary	E.	Lanny McDonald	66 goals — 1982-83
4.	Chicago	L.	Bobby Hull	58 goals — 1968-69
5.	Colorado	H.	Michel Goulet	57 goals — 1982-83
6.	Detroit	G.	Steve Yzerman	65 goals — 1988-89
7.	Edmonton	K.	Wayne Gretzky	92 goals — 1981-82
8.	Montreal	P.	Guy Lafleur	60 goals — 1976-77
9.	NYR	M.	Adam Graves	52 goals — 1993-94
10.	Ottawa	B.	Alexei Yashin	44 goals — 1998-99
11.	Philadelphia	N.	Reggie Leach	61 goals — 1975-76
12.	Pittsburgh	D.	Mario Lemieux	85 goals — 1988-89
13.	St. Louis	A.	Brett Hull	86 goals — 1990-91
14.	Toronto	O.	Rick Vaive	54 goals — 1981-82
15.	Vancouver	F.	Pavel Bure	60 goals — 1992-93
16.	Washington	J.	Dennis Maruk	60 goals — 1981-82

ACKNOWLEDGEMENTS

Thanks to the following publishers and organizations for the use of photographs and quoted and statistical material:

Associated Press AP. Carlos Osorio (photo, page 11), 1998.

The *Calgary Herald*. Larry MacDougall (photo, page 104), 1998.

The *Dallas Morning News*. Burl Osborne.

The *Hockey News,* various excerpts. Reprinted by permission of the *Hockey News*, a division of GTC, Transcontinental Publishing, Inc.

The *National Post*. The *National Post*.

Total Hockey. Dan Diamond and Associates, Inc. Total Sports, 1998.

Care has been taken to trace ownership of copyright material contained in this book. The publishers welcome any information that will enable them to rectify any reference or credit in subsequent editions.

The author gratefully acknowledges the help of Gary Meagher and Benny Ercolani of the NHL; Phil Prichard, Craig Campbell and Jeff Davis at the Hockey Hall of Fame; Peter Brosseau at the *Calgary Herald*; the sports broadcasters at CFCF 12 in Montreal; the staff at the McLellan-Redpath Library at McGill University; Rob Sanders, Terri Wershler and Leanne Denis at Greystone Books; the many hockey writers and broadcasters who have made the game better through their own work; my Webmaster, Mike Curran; fact checker Allen Bishop, who is better at finding mistakes than making them; editors Kerry Banks and Anne Rose, who literally climb mountains (to Neil's place) to get the job done; and graphic artist Peter van Vlaardingen and puzzle designer Adrian van Vlaardingen for their outstanding work.

HOCKEY TRIVIA'S READER REBOUND

Do you have a favourite hockey trivia question? Write us, and if we haven't used it before, we may include your question in next year's trivia book. We'll make sure every question selected is credited with the sender's name and city. Sorry, we can't answer letters individually.

Write us at: *Hockey Trivia*
c/o Don Weekes
P.O. Box 221
Montreal, Quebec
Canada   H4A 3P5

PLEASE PRINT

NAME: _____ AGE: _____

ADDRESS: _____

YOUR QUESTION: _____

_____

_____

_____

_____

_____

_____

ANSWER: _____

_____

_____

_____

_____

_____

_____

_____

_____